LIFE AT SCHOOL

By the same author

Achieving a Ph.D
Psychology in the Classroom

LIFE AT SCHOOL

Education and Psychology

Phillida Salmon

Constable · London

First published in Great Britain by Constable and Company Limited 1998
3 The Lanchesters, 162 Fulham Palace Road, London W6 9ER

Copyright © Phillida Salmon 1998
ISBN 0 09 477450 1
The right of Phillida Salmon to be identified as the author of this work has
been asserted by her in accordance with the Copyright, Designs and
Patents Act 1988
Set in Linotype Sabon 10½pt by SetSystems Ltd, Saffron Walden
Printed in Great Britain by St Edmundsbury Press Ltd
Bury St Edmunds, Suffolk

A CIP catalogue record for this book is available from the British Library

Contents

Acknowledgements

I am grateful to Carol O'Brien for her light touch as editor, and to David Smail for suggesting and encouraging this book. Viv Burr offered characteristically insightful comments and suggestions. As always, Sheila Macrae proved a helpful and generous resource. My greatest debt is to my friend Ann Phoenix, for her loving support and her constancy.

I

Introduction

What kind of psychology underpins our system of schooling? What are the assumptions about children and young people, about learning and teaching, that make us organise education in the way we do? These are questions with which we are all, to some extent, concerned. Education is something everyone knows about in some sense. There are very few adults who have not experienced some form of schooling. Many are involved, directly or indirectly, in the educational system. Currently, this system rates high on the political agenda; scarcely a week goes by without some new ruling or pronouncement from the government. Messages are constantly beamed at the constituency of parents, as the 'consumers' in the education market.

If the schooling system is currently a high-profile topic, this is because it is seen to be a problematic one. Failing schools, incompetent teachers, and poor educational standards feature almost daily in the mass media. Drastic steps, we are told, must be taken to bring things up to scratch. There will be regular and stringent monitoring by the Office for Standards in Education. In the worst scenario, whole schools will be closed down. Inefficient heads will be replaced, poor teachers sacked. Standards will be rigorously maintained by tight central control of the curriculum and of teaching methods.

Many of those at the receiving end of this rhetoric may feel a sense of bemusement. Probably few people would disagree with the idea that in many ways our schooling system falls short. The evidence of this is hard to deny, for pupils offer their own clear testimony. The high rate of truancy, the disruptive behaviour in classrooms, the falling behind of whole groups of children: these things speak of an educational system that is failing to engage a high proportion of its clients. Yet for many parents, and other concerned adults, what is wrong is not simply a matter of failure on the part of teachers to inculcate certain measurable skills. The problem will be not remedied by attention to academic aspects alone. It has to do with the whole quality of children's school experience.

One of the basic assumptions underlying formal education is that its benefits lie in the future. We see schooling in essentially preparatory terms: as training children for their lives as adults, as equipping them with the skills they will need for employment, parenthood, maturity. From this point of view, their present experience hardly matters in itself; what counts is the degree to which it contributes to a future that is rewarding for themselves and their society. To children themselves, and to those who care about them, this is surely a strange way to see things – for the 15,000 hours of compulsory schooling constitute a major proportion of human life. This paradoxical feature is the topic of Chapter 2 in this book.

Other chapters question some equally basic assumptions about the function of schooling. Some of these have to do with the meaning of age and its progression. Our education system is geared to the idea that development proceeds in a regular and continuous way as the years of childhood pass. This idea governs the classroom groupings of children by age, on the one hand, and, on the other, the progressive changes in the curriculum of lessons from infant to primary, from primary to secondary. But assumptions about children's development do themselves need to be looked at critically, for although we conventionally believe that thinking proceeds from concrete to abstract, it may be that the most advanced forms of thought are in fact grounded within human particulars. And children do not, perhaps, learn in a gradual, step-wise fashion; indeed, very young children seem capable of far greater understanding than we generally assume.

Any discussion of education must concern itself with how it is that children come to develop intellectually. We usually see this as a simple question of learning. Tailored to the gradual acquisition of knowledge, of particular kinds of understanding, our schooling system seems to provide the necessary medium for intellectual growth. Perhaps, though, we should look at things differently. For thinking is essentially active; it involves initiative. The passive and receptive role demanded of pupils in school can only be inimical to this sort of development.

Thinking is itself fundamental to learning. Yet the way that learning is generally assessed leaves little room for this, tending to focus on purely mechanical aspects. Such measurements are far from incidental; they have heavy consequences. For young people, they carry all the implications of labelling, for present placements and for future destinies. Nor are they immaterial for schools, since institutional viability depends upon position in the league tables.

These features are all fundamental to the explicit functions of schooling, yet for young people and their parents they may in the end prove less important than the social aspects of school experience. Personal relationships with teachers and with fellow pupils are conventionally viewed as largely irrelevant to education. Only when they prove impossibly problematic do they become the focus of attention. The organisation of the school regime makes no room for these features. The curriculum of lessons is remote from such matters, which are relegated, if they are addressed at all, to the increasingly marginalised sphere of personal and social education. Despite all this, the personal encounters that young people have with each other, and with their teachers, often have a momentous significance – a significance that may govern attitudes to schooling itself.

Though our education system does not, officially, include inter-personal relationships in its curriculum, nevertheless schools teach their own lessons about personal status and social relations. Through what has been called the hidden curriculum, pupils receive clear messages about these fundamental aspects of human life. Typically, these messages endorse the unequal status of different groups within our own society. Among these, the inequities of gender may be particularly important; and it is to these inequities that two chapters of this book are addressed.

So long as the inexplicit functions of schooling remain unquestioned, our educational institution are likely – unwittingly – to perpetuate the kinds of oppression that operate within the wider society. But in corners of the system, many teachers are already working to change practice. As illustrated throughout this book, there are places in the world of school where things are being done differently. Despite the bureaucratic and political pressures on teaching, the lack of books and resources, the crumbling fabric of school buildings, some of the unlikeliest young people are blossoming.

For all the difficulties under which they daily labour, there are some teachers who refuse to operate the narrow limitations of formal schooling; who convey a personal recognition of their pupils and their pupils' lives; and who create in their classroom an atmosphere of affirmation and respect.

The schooling system that this book addresses is not the only one in our society. Some readers may have experienced a very different kind of education: one within the private sector. This sphere differs in many ways from that governed by local authorities. Privately funded schools have richer resources, and a selective intake; they can take for granted standards that may be difficult to achieve in the public system. To that extent, many aspects of the schooling discussed here may be unfamiliar to such readers. Yet the fundamental assumptions that govern how we see children and their development – the psychology that underpins the kind of education we offer – may not itself be very different across the two spheres. It is this psychology that is the essential focus of this book; and the context in which it is debated here is chosen because it is the one in which most children experience it today.

2

The Ideology of Schooling

For many parents, their children's daytime lives represent an unknown quantity. School is a world apart. If this is generally less the case for the infant and early primary years, the sense of separateness will certainly have intensified by the secondary stage. Of course efforts are made on both sides to bridge this general gulf. There are few parents who do not try to learn as much as they can about their children's schooling: the advantages and disadvantages of particular schools, their children's progress as learners, the subject choices they must take, the problems they experience, and so on. Yet for most people struggling on behalf of their children, the routines, the demands, even the language of schooling, can often seem mysterious and opaque.

For their part, head teachers are necessarily concerned to establish and maintain good home–school relations. For some parents, mothers in particular, there is direct access of a sort through work as classroom or playground assistants, or, at a grander level, as parent governors. But these encounters with the world of school are necessarily limited and partial, involving aspects that may be of marginal significance to their children. In principle, contact with school and teachers for all parents is guaranteed by regular open days and parents' meetings. However, these occasions do not necessarily benefit those for whom the home–school gulf is at its widest. Those whose conditions of employment are inflexible may be unable to attend meetings. For many, there is a sense of discomfort in communicating with teachers. In general, it is middle-class parents who are able to put such opportunities to some use, while working-class parents and minority group members may simply find them alienating.

We have all been children; and it is to their own experience as pupils that most adults probably turn in trying to grasp the school worlds their children now inhabit. Yet the way things were twenty years ago constitutes only a shaky guide to today's classroom realities. Of course in certain fundamentals the institution of schooling has remained the same, but even within a single generation there have been major changes. The whole educational system has been reorganised. Local authorities, previously influential, have been marginalised. The inspection service has been privatised. Head teachers have been allocated managerial control of their schools. With the creation of differently resourced grant-maintained schools and city technology colleges, supposedly comprehensive secondary education is being quietly eroded.

Nor, with the imposition of a National Curriculum, is the content of classroom learning exempt from its own revolution. As part of this, the public monitoring of attainment, previously reserved for examination at age sixteen, has now invaded the learning of children even at primary level, with key stages to be achieved at seven, eleven and fourteen. And it is not only formal aspects of school life that have undergone change: schools themselves are apparently in crisis. Low educational standards and 'failing' schools are a matter of national concern. Problems of indiscipline, disruption and classroom violence are constantly paraded before the public.

Issues such as these are at the forefront of political debate and media interest. There is currently a great deal of noise being made about schools. The constituency of parents is daily targeted: cajoled, exhorted, threatened. In the supposed free market of the schooling system, they are to be the customers. Wanting the best for their children, today's men and women struggle to make the right decisions. Yet schools themselves, the contexts on which so much, it seems, depends, remain remote, a world in which as adults they have no place. Unless they teach or perform some other institutional function, parents have no business there. They cannot be accommodated, except as occasional marginal onlookers. Nor can their children bridge the gulf. While in the early years of schooling young pupils may bring their parents in on their school lives at least to some extent, as the years progress communication, on both sides, becomes increasingly impossible.

Probably all parents feel regretful, at least sometimes, about their ignorance of their children's schooltime lives. Perhaps few people, though, would question the fundamental distinctions on which it rests. We take for granted the separation between children and adults, and see it as natural that they should inhabit different worlds. The institution of schooling, catering as it does for the nature of childhood, is, we generally assume, no more suited to mature people than the world of full-time paid employment is to an eight-year-old girl. Unlike earlier generations, we recognise the distinctive character of childishness – we let children be children, rather than forcing them prematurely into adult roles. Compulsory mass schooling, as embodying this recognition, is something we take pride in.

Work and school. These social institutions seem in complementary ways, to reflect and cater for the different needs of adults on the one hand, and children on the other. Just as grown men and women have moved beyond the stage of formalised learning, so young people are as yet unready to enter the world of paid employment. Work, as we generally see it, entails capacities that, by definition, children have still to acquire: capacities of understanding, competence and social responsibility. (This is not to say that many adult jobs would themselves justify such attributions.) But above every other sphere of human activity, paid employment seems incompatible with the essential unseriousness of childhood. So basic is this assumption that, as Virginia Morrow (1994) argues, we fail to see that by the early secondary years most young people are already actively particpating in the labour market.

Morrow herself has made a study of children's work. Within a large sample of British eleven- to sixteen-year-olds, she finds involvement in work to be typical rather than exceptional. Quite often this entails part-time waged labour in the service sector or in newspaper delivery. Sometimes work is of a more informal kind: babysitting, odd jobs involving domestic or car maintenance tasks. Other young people participate in the family business. In all these cases, though, the work done represents a real contribution to the socio-economic world. Far from being something frivolous – a mere playing at working – these young people, and those who employ them, take their activity entirely seriously. It is on their capability, their competence, their commitment, that the employment contract depends.

To children themselves, the genuine involvement in the adult world that employment confers is something highly prized. This is obviously in part because money allows the purchase of clothes, the opportunity to go out with friends, and so on. But perhaps it is not merely a question of financial reward as such. Colin Ward (1994), a lifelong champion of young people's autonomy, believes that the independent earnings that work affords are in the end less important than its social accolade. Because economic 'pulling power' is accorded unqualified respect in our society, children as workers can meet the adult world on equal terms.

To most parents, the generality of young people's involvement in work of some kind would hardly come as a revelation. Their own child's part-time job, the early morning figure cycling or trudging by with its heavy yellow plastic bag: there are daily reminders of the ubiquitousness of children's employment. Yet somehow the implications of this engagement remain unassimilated within our ideas about childhood. In our psychology of young life, we still persist in defining children as unready for 'real' work, and as fit only for a preparatory role.

Morrow's study suggests that, in one important respect at least, our picture of childhood is out of keeping with practical realities. So ingrained, it seems, is our assumption that children are constitutionally unready for work, that in our everyday view of them we are virtually blind to the fact of their considerable existing involvement. Work is perhaps the touchstone of adulthood, of maturity. If on this aspect we fail to see how things actually are, our whole conception of the nature of childhood as fundamentally different from adulthood may need to be reconsidered.

Rather than defining children as essentially different from adults, we might instead begin with their basic human commonality. This would of course be a revolutionary thing to do. To current consciousness, questioning the crucial difference between childhood and maturity seems absurd. Surely we know, from decades of scientific research, that young people are qualitatively distinct? Have they not been shown, through many well-respected studies, to think differently from adults, to see things in their own, different terms, to live in an essentially pre-adult world?

These supposed 'findings' are apparently unquestionable. Yet scientific knowledge, though it seems objective, is in fact deeply embedded within prevailing contemporary arrangements. The same social structures, the same institutional practices, that reflect and endorse ordinary 'common sense', also underpin the activities that we call research. It is precisely this intertwining of theoretical understanding and everyday ways of doing things that makes it so difficult to call our assumptions into question. Because these assumptions are endorsed both by professional knowledge and by everyday understanding, they seem undeniably true. 'They comprise the fabric of ourselves and our relationships that constitute our very subjectivity.' So speaks Erica Burman (1994), a psychologist much concerned to challenge our usual understanding of childhood. Along with a growing number of people, Burman urges a critical re-examination of the way we see children and their childishness.

Our psychology of childhood is, unsurprisingly, a psychology evolved by men and women rather than by children themselves. It is written, as it were, from the standpoint of adults. Because of this, it views young people in terms of their difference from 'us'. Seen from this perspective, children are necessarily lesser. Our understanding centres upon what they *cannot* do: on their incapacities, their incompleteness, their not-yet status.

The indisputability of this characterisation seems borne out by a multitude of ordinary daily experiences. While grown-up people participate in the 'real world', children, so we think, lead their own separate, childish lives. Women and men contribute to the economy; children merely depend on it. The world's serious business is not carried out by the young. It is adults who work, draw income support, manage households; children can only work and play. Contrary evidence, such as Morrow's study, remains invisible, so apparent does all this seem. Childhood, by definition, involves ignorance, dependence, vulnerability, irresponsibility. All this is recognised, of course, in legal provision. Disqualification from full-time work, sexual intercourse, marriage, electoral duties, army service or criminal liability embodies taken-for-granted assumptions about the lesser status of children.

As many writers have now acknowledged, present-day notions of childhood have only a short history. It was the pioneering work of the French historian Philippe Ariès that for most people first revealed the very different lives led by children in Europe a few centuries ago. During the Middle Ages, for instance, there were no divisions in kind between the young and their elders. Even the youngest children took part in just the same activities as the men and women around them. They dressed in similar clothes, ate and slept together, and made their own contribution to the household economy. The child barriers we ourselves erect in spheres of work and leisure, our special arenas for adults only, were then quite unknown.

If current ideas about children are themselves historically relative, they are also specific to our own particular society and culture. Images of the Third World show us very different sorts of childhood. To quote Burman again, 'There are many non-Western children leading responsible, autonomous and far from carefree lives.' Clearly, our ideas about childhood and our treatment of children do not reflect some universal truth about young life. Instead, they are the product of our own particular society.

School is the world where, willy-nilly, girls and boys must spend many years of their lives, but in a number of important ways it is not their world. The lesser status of the young is nowhere more evident than in the institutional arrangements of the schooling system. Most fundamentally, attendance itself is compulsory. Children are not asked whether they wish to come to school; personal choice is not on offer. The evident disinclination of many young people could in fact significantly reduce the school population, were such choices available. But contracts, the option currently under political consideration, are not to be signed by pupils, but by their parents. The recipients of schooling are not themselves regarded as responsible agents, but instead as passive beneficiaries of adults acting on their behalf.

To most of us, all this seems perfectly natural. We take it for granted that children, being children, cannot yet know their own best interests. Left to themselves, they would be likely to make foolish choices, to act on the basis of ignorant, frivolous or short-term considerations. It is surely better to leave vital decisions about their lives to knowledgeable and concerned adults who have their best interests at heart.

School, in popular understanding, represents a parallel with work: the one for children, the other for adults. But one has only to consider the very different provisions made for human rights in these two arenas to realise the significantly lower status accorded to the young. The contract between working men and women, on the one hand, and their employers on the other, allows for a withdrawal of labour. Pupils, of course, have no such right. Absence from work is not without adverse consequences; there may be loss of earnings, even dismissal, but it is not a criminal offence. For a school absentee, however, truancy is a criminalised act; it carries legal sanctions, penalties. Nor do pupils have collective rights. Working people, through their trade unions, may legitimately act to improve working conditions and resist exploitation. School councils, where they exist, do offer young people at least some degree of responsibility. But these

are not the norm, and, because they work against the institutional grain, often represent mere tokens of democracy. In
general, children in school have no access to any such
collective representation.

To many people this situation would appear perfectly
justifiable. The position of pupils, they might say, is in the
end fundamentally different from that of workers. Office
cleaners, factory hands, retailers, financiers: they all contribute to society. The work they do has social value. That, of
course, is why they get paid. What children do at school, on
the other hand, is of no benefit except to themselves; it will
qualify them for a job when they come to leave school.

Quite another point of view is put forward by Jens Qvortrup (1991), a Danish sociologist and member of a European
research centre. Pupils' school work, so Qvortrup argues, not
merely benefits the wider world; it is socially vital. Society
can function only if it has an effective labour force; and this
depends on producing and accumulating knowledge: the task
with which children, together with their teachers, are engaged.
As Qvortrup puts it, 'the production of knowledge is a pre-
requisite for the functioning of a modern economy'. From this
standpoint, children's schoolwork, despite the fact that it goes
unrewarded, has undeniable social exchange value.

To take this sort of perspective would be to question the
lack of agency and the deprivation of responsibility that go
with pupil status. If we saw classroom work as contributing
significantly to society, we should expect the schooling system to make children partners in the enterprise, rather than
merely products of it. But this is not, of course, the way we
generally view things. We take for granted the passive status
accorded to young people in school because it fits in with
our ideas about children as still unready for social
responsibility.

Yet there is something strange about this child psychology.

Certainly it sits oddly with the lives that children lead at home. To parents, even babies seem to have a will of their own; they are hardly passive creatures to be easily moulded by the actions of others. From their earliest years, boys and girls make their active presence, their wilful agency, their demands and protests, very vividly felt. In every household that has children, negotiations must be made with young family members; their personal agendas have somehow to be accommodated. These are not the helpless, dependent beings that supposedly define childhood.

The contrasting lives that children lead at home and at school are a central focus of concern for Berry Mayall. In a recent study, she talked to two groups of children at an inner-city primary school: five-year-olds and nine-year-olds. Their experience within the two contexts, as emerges from what they say, is markedly different. Even at the age of five, these children are clearly taking an active part in family life: 'Children do not just belong to the family; they, to an extent, together with other family members, continuously create the family. They construct and refine relationships and social customs, and negotiate the division of labour within the home, settling conditionally for duties and freedoms, and renegotiating these over time' (Mayall, 1994, p. 63). For both age groups, other family members deal with them as particular individuals, and recognise their ability, and their right, to exercise some responsibility over their own lives. The authority of adults is mediated by these kinds of awareness.

Things are very different at school. Here, Mayall's subjects tell her, there is little scope for negotiation. Conformity with pre-established rules is the norm; challenging adult authority is not legitimate. Children have little power to reconstruct or modify their classroom worlds. The schooling system, argues Mayall, is so built as to ensure that young people never reach maturity and independence. The competence and the self-reliance children have acquired at home goes unrecognised within an educational setting that disallows initiative and choice.

As will be evident in later chapters of this book, schooling is not quite the monolithic entity of Mayall's portrayal. There is room there for a good deal more negotiation between teachers and pupils than her argument suggests. As much good practice has demonstrated, school can be made a place where young people find respect, and at least some room for their own agendas. But such practice has to work against the grain. The institutional nature of schooling necessarily means that life there is not easily negotiable.

If schools, in their daily dealings with pupils, operate on the basis of one kind of psychology, it seems that parents typically relate to their children in terms of a rather different one. They treat their sons and daughters not as helpless incompetents, but as human beings with the same capacity for likes and dislikes, for personal decisions, for co-operation and resistance as they possess themselves. By contrast, the institution of schooling, deriving from a picture of children as different and lesser, maintains a view of education as a preparation for life, rather than as life itself.

The not-yet status that, in our general understanding of childhood, we accord the young carries an implicit devaluation of children as children. It sees childhood as on the way, as a stage preliminary to membership of a world that belongs to adults. From this point of view, it is schooling that guarantees full membership of that world. By instilling in its recipients, through their youthful years, the necessary skills and knowledge, formal education will prepare them for their adult roles as citizens, employees, parents.

Children are often referred to as the future generation. They are seen as 'our' future, in a phrase that seems to deny their present value, their intrinsic value for themselves. In this philosophy they are defined not as beings, but as becomings. Yet for their parents, young people are intensely, undeniably, present in the here and now; and their importance as people is by no means to be reduced to their future status as adults. Parents care for sons and daughters as the children they still are, even, perhaps, regretting the all-too-fleeting passage of childhood.

But if those who live with children experience them in the present tense, it is their future prospects that define their school existence. We see education, essentially, as preparatory, as relevant to an adulthood not yet arrived at. Our evaluation of schooling rests on its capacity to qualify for the period that we call maturity. Learning is taken to mean accreditation for adult life. The key stages that represent the current way-stations of achievement at three- or four-year intervals take their significance as steps towards that all-important testing place: the GCSE, or, in Scotland, the School Leaving Certificate. The index of an individual school's success, its claims in the stakes of parental choice, rests in the end upon its proven capacity to accredit.

As will be evident later, exam qualification is not the simple passport to employment that we generally suppose. Nevertheless, unqualified young adults do not get very far in our society. Enabling its pupils to pass exams is certainly important for any school, but surely that is not its only function. School is a place where girls and boys will spend, in Michael Rutter's phrase, 15,000 hours of their lives (Rutter *et al.*, 1979). Within that long stretch of existence, it can offer friendship, interest, a sense of potential – or loneliness, fear and alienation. Living, as we all do, in the here and now, young people react intensely to their contemporary surroundings. For some pupils, school is a congenial world, a life enjoyed, something looked forward to. For others it becomes a hated place, to be escaped in whatever ways prove possible.

Caring as they do for their offspring, most parents are acutely aware of the potential for happiness or misery that schools entail. Their children's contentment and sense of well-being rank high among the criteria on which they make their choices. Will he fit in, feel at home here? Will she make friends, get on with children from such different backgrounds? As a child of mixed parentage in an almost all-white school, will he suffer racist abuse? These are questions parents necessarily ask themselves in comparing school possibilities. And this is true not only at the primary stage; even in the secondary sector, where exam success is ostensibly at a premium, their children's well-being remains supremely important.

This book sets out to examine schooling in the present, rather than the usual future tense. Its concern is not with education as preparation, but with school life as currently lived experience. In order to do this, it will be necessary to look closely, critically, at a psychology that has generally prevented us from attending to young people in the here and now. It is because our understanding of childhood rests on a conception of children as not-yet adults that our perspectives on schooling have taken so little account of school life as it is actually lived. This has meant that educational realities have been typically reduced to a single dimension, that cognitive aspects have been over-emphasised at the expense of social and personal ones, and that the huge complexity of classroom encounters has been largely overlooked.

Our conventional psychology of childhood rests on the idea of development as a natural, inborn progression that moves through certain universal stages. We believe this occurs within all the major spheres of human functioning:

intellectual, moral, social. In each of these arenas there is, we think, a pinnacle, a final point to be reached, which is that of adulthood, maturity.

All this seems no more than common sense, but looking closely at the evidence may suggest other interpretations. At first glance young people in school seem to fit neatly into our image of development. There they are, at six, talking like six-year-olds, doing just the things we know six-year-olds do. Five years later, their talk, their activities, are of a clearly different order; they are recognisably the pre-adolescent children of every textbook. Move on another five years, and you have typical adolescents: a different species again. All this seems to happen of its own accord, through some pre-existing, pre-ordained developmental pattern. But it is, perhaps, precisely through the social customs, the institutional arrangements that derive from our own assumptions about childhood, that children come to 'develop' in the particular ways that they do.

Human functioning, though we often think of it as biologically determined, is ultimately the outcome of human culture. What we call maturation is by no means the simple unfolding of innate developmental patterns. If that were so, we should see it repeated across the centuries and over widely different societies. How children come to grow and change is very much a function of the social expectations, the social opportunities, that surround them. Though we may believe that we 'discover' the changes of childhood, in fact they are the product of our own human activity. That is the argument put forward by John Morss (1996), a psychologist who sets out to challenge the whole idea of development. As human beings, he suggests, we continually make and remake each other's lives: 'We think we read each other, and forget that we write each other.'

To look at things in this way means seeing schooling and

school experience very differently. As a major arena in young life, where pupils meet their teachers and each other in often fateful encounters, the school context carries great power in the construction of children's identities and personal func tioning. Though our conventional understanding and our institutional arrangements typically deny it, the social learn ing that school teaches is every bit as significant as its cognitive legacy.

If the social importance of schooling is generally underes-timated, there are many teachers for whom it is all too apparent. These are people who struggle to put classroom learning to positive social use: to respect the identities of their pupils, to widen access to 'really useful knowledge', to enlarge mutual appreciation across the divides of gender, race and class. Such efforts on the part of teachers, which will feature in this book's discussion, illustrate the implica-tions of taking school life as important in the now, rather than merely for the future. For it is the huge present signific-ance for pupils of their schooling experience that represents the central theme of this book.

3

School as Institution

In school, says Peter Woods, 'pupils are engaged in a continual battle for who they are and who they are to become, while the forces of institutionalisation work to deprive them of their individuality' (Woods, 1977, p. 248). This picture is one that most young people would recognise. For many pupils, school means a sense of anonymity, of personal lostness in a mass of others. For crowds are a prime feature of schooling; vast numbers assemble and mill about, to the accompaniment of deafening noise and physical jostling – 'frantic passengers', as David Hargreaves (1975) puts it, 'in an over-crowded airport'. The schedules of the schooling system and its curriculum delivery function require that young people en masse come together and stay in one place, engaged in specified activities for specified lengths of time. Bureaucratic necessity leaves little room for manoeuvre for pupils – or even for teachers.

Being in a crowd is one of the defining features of school. In this context it is almost impossible to be alone, to find even a few minutes' solitude in a quiet corner. The long school day offers little respite from the pressures of mass regimentation. For pressures there are: crowds do not generally make a comfortable milieu. Whereas friendship groups are bound together by mutual liking and support, schooling groups are arbitrarily thrown together. Their major common denominator is age, and sometimes gender. Home locality may also be shared. But essentially they cut across existing friendships and alliances. Age alone they have in common, and perhaps defined ability level. Against the stresses, the anxieties, the hurtful encounters of school life, they offer little personal protection. For a minority, the 'kings of the school', the gang represents a context of personal recognition. But for every winner, there are many more losers – young people who feel alone and vulnerable in the heaving numbers in the playground or the lunch hall. This lonely crowd bestows no sense of collective belonging, but only anonymity and alienation.

The mass treatment of young people, which is one consequence of school bureaucracy, has its own built-in paradoxes. For pupils and teachers alike, the sheer volume of human beings involved in classroom work is a source of frustration. To be treated as just another group member, as no more than a number, is something young people bitterly resent; and many children go right through their school lives without ever feeling that any adult recognises them as individuals. For some, one-to-one encounters with their teachers are few and far between. This is particularly true of 'middle-of-the road' pupils, those whose unexceptional, and unexceptionable, conduct and performance allows them to be ignored in favour of academically able, 'special needs', or simply disruptive classmates. For reasons to be discussed later in this book, such pupils are especially likely to be girls. For their part, teachers face growing class sizes that make it virtually impossible to give adequate attention to the needs of so many charges. The crowdedness of school, it seems, is a feature that no one there endorses.

In their classrooms, children sit close together, side by side at tables or at desks near others. There is little privacy in such proximity; pupils have easy access to each other's work. Yet the schooling system is based on learning as individualised. Though group work is regularly practised by teachers at both primary and secondary levels, any work written in exercise books must be done by pupils on their own. And significantly, the assessment and accreditation of learning applies to pupils as individual learners. Hearing the questions of classmates, seeing their neighbours' written responses, pupils are nevertheless required to ignore the learning efforts all around them, and to function, somehow, as isolated units. Co-operative work, unless specifically called for, is disallowed; children quickly learn that 'cheating' is severely proscribed.

Despite the problems it creates for both pupils and their teachers, and in apparent defiance of its own logic of learning as individualised, the institution of schooling rests upon a herding together of children. The psychology that underpins this practice is one that divorces intellectual functioning from social aspects, and sees its development as age-related. If a school class is defined by the common age of its members, it is because this feature, supposedly governing the level of young people's cognitive development, is seen as solely relevant to the modes and content of their learning. It is convenient, therefore, to aggregate pupils of similar ages, so that they can receive an identical learning curriculum. The learning process itself, however, as a solitary endeavour, is not thought to require any reference to the minds of other learners. And if classroom groupings ride roughshod over existing friendships and alliances, this does not matter, since school is unconcerned with pupils' social relationships, except where they cause problems.

As institutions, schools are not merely asocial places in which to be; they are, in some senses, positively anti-social. It is not just that they do not set out to foster the development of mutual appreciation and respect between pupils; to some extent they actually undermine such development. The culture of individualism that, under current political pressures, increasingly defines their ways of functioning, is a culture where many must go to the wall. When not merely pupils, but even schools themselves, are set in competition, one against the other, losers will outnumber winners. In competitive school learning, with its ever earlier grading system, even the most able children achieve their position at a cost. Not merely is there further to fall; the top of the hierarchy is reached through a process that entails a growing alienation from schoolmates less academically inclined.

The schooling system, as Berry Mayall (1994) puts it, treats its pupils not as valued persons, but as projects. The essential business of education, as built into its institutional structures, is the acquisition of knowledge, without regard to the personal identities of those who are to acquire it. So dominant is this concern that it can sometimes undermine practices set up to counter its effects. The pastoral care system, now a universal feature of schooling, is one example. In principle this system embodies humane treatment, and guarantees caring and respectful recognition for every pupil. But because its rationale is not seen as educational, pastoral care tends to operate in a vacuum, separated from the classroom demands and pressures, the stressful daily encounters that give rise to so many young people's school problems. The same predominance of narrowly defined educational goals can also encroach on the essential functions of this system. Overwhel med as they increasingly are both with administrative and with disciplinary duties, teachers who double as pastoral care staff can often find little space for genuine pastoral work.

If, as Woods believes, schooling entails for its students a constant, often unsuccessful, struggle to be recognised, this is surely because the position of pupil is one of massive subordination. Learning to be a pupil means above all learning to submit to teachers. This is how Mary Willes (1983) depicts things, as a result of her many careful observations and interviews in inner-city infant classrooms. Even by the age of four, she records, young children are already expected to behave in highly submissive ways that are most unlike their ordinary conduct. An early, fundamental lesson is learning how to bid. Wanting to say something, a pupil may not speak, but only indicate the wish to do so by raising a hand, and waiting attentively. On the teacher's nomination ('Yes, Daniel?', 'No, not you, Sharon') the chosen speaker responds, briefly, and then awaits the teacher's evaluation of the utterance.

The control that teachers possess over their interchanges with even the youngest children includes the right to dictate what it is appropriate to say. Their evaluations are likely to include some reference to relevance: a concept, Willes suggests, that most four-year-olds have yet to learn: 'They know they have to give short responses to the teacher's questions, but they are not very good at guessing what sort of answers will be acceptable ... Nor do they recognise yet that the right to change the topic belongs to the teacher and to nobody else in the room' (Willes, 1983, pp. 78–9).

Most features of this essentially subordinate pupil role have to be absorbed by osmosis; few, even the most fundamental, are explicitly taught. Some aspects are quite subtle. Classroom business, as Willes sees it, depends on pupils demonstrating, on demand, what it is they know. It also entails being able to read between the lines, in grasping teachers' meanings: 'to recognise negative evaluation on the part of the teacher for what it is, even when it is indirectly expressed' (Willes, 1983, p. 84). But this is all part of a much wider lesson: that of teachers' overwhelming classroom power.

The subordination of young people in school settings is nowhere more evident than in the grossly unequal ratio of pupil/teacher talk. As Willes argues, in classrooms it is adults rather than children who have conversational rights. Teachers hugely out-talk pupils. Teachers may interrupt, but not be interrupted. Where pupils do speak, this is often to elicit teacher directives – 'What do I do when I've finished this?', 'Can I have a rubber?', and so on. Schooling, so Willes argues, quickly teaches children that the most acceptable responses are monosyllabic.

The all-powerful figures in this classroom scene are, of course, entirely illusory. Today's teachers are anything but free agents. Hemmed in by numerous official and unofficial pressures and directives, overloaded with endless administrative and bureaucratic duties, subject to constantly changing demands, teaching staff are themselves very far from autonomous beings. Nevertheless, in the experience of pupils, classrooms belong not to them, but to their teachers.

For young people, it is the denial of their own competence, responsibility and initiative that features most strongly in resentment and frustration towards the schooling system. Even for children starting school, as Berry Mayall suggests, the part they are called upon to play is one that insultingly ignores the self-reliance, the capacity to make decisions, that they have already achieved: 'Being refused permission to go to the toilet or get a drink can be distressing. So can sitting in a noisy hall eating food you have had no part in choosing' (Mayall, 1994, p. 56).

At the other end of the age scale, in the later secondary years, the pupil role contrasts still more starkly with the relative social freedom accorded to young people out of school. To Andy Hargreaves and colleagues writing about this stage of education, the restrictions and general passivity demanded of learners is borne of anxiety as to the potentially unsettling effects of their energies: 'Adolescent energy can seem to us organisationally dangerous and imminently over-powering, so we organise learning individually, statically and sedentarily so as to restrain it' (Hargreaves *et al.*, 1996, p. 13).

The institutional system of schools takes little account of the social maturity of the girls and boys for whom it caters. The whole day is pre-organised, with little space for pupils to make choices or decide things for themselves. Learners are expected to be passive rather than show initiative: to sit quietly, listening to their teachers, and obediently switch attention at the ringing of a bell. What often makes all this still worse is the environment itself. Decaying buildings, leaking roofs, toilets with no locks, poorly heated and venti-lated classrooms convey clear messages of disrespect. That these features are resented by young people is evident from a recent study carried out by Jean Rudduck with a number of colleagues (1996), in which she asks secondary pupils for their views on schooling.

As Rudduck argues, young people themselves are seldom consulted about their schooling. Typically they are seen merely as its passive beneficiaries. Little attention is paid to their experience; their critiques are rarely sought, let alone acted on. Yet, as insiders, intimately familiar with every detail of school practice, pupils represent a valuable resource and, potentially, an agency for positive change.

It is just in these terms that many of the pupils in this study express themselves. When their teachers treat them with respect, as partners in the enterprise, this is much appreciated. Being wholly dominated, on the other hand, being subject to the authoritarian exercise of power, is something bitterly resented. This is sometimes felt in the arbitrary imposition of petty rules: 'not being allowed to eat outside even if we're swamped in the dining room'. Excessive homework, encroaching on legitimate personal and social concerns, can represent another instance. This is still more likely to be the case if it is demanded pointlessly, just for its own sake: 'You've done it in class and when you go home it's just to do the same thing, and you already know it'.

Yet there are also positives in these young people's school experience. Trips and other out-of-school activities are discussed with real enthusiasm. Nor are these events merely time out. Pupils talk of what they learn on these occasions: a learning that seems personally meaningful, a learning that will be remembered. In classroom work, too, it is the space made for their own activity, their own initiative, their own control, that these young people most appreciate: practicals, project work, small group discussion or collaborative learning.

Such activities can take place only in a classroom context where initial inequalities of power have been at least partly moderated. Most fundamentally, this involves a negotiation between teachers and their pupils. Classroom order depends on the establishment of a working consensus between the two sides. In this, not just the teacher's agenda, but the interests, energies and limitations of pupils, must be allowed for, taken into account.

When young people, at whatever stage of schooling, talk about their teachers, what they almost invariably emphasise as important is fairness and consistency. For any classroom order to work, pupils have to know where they stand. Departures from implicitly agreed ways of behaving are undermining. A teacher who behaves unreasonably, by being arbitrary, reprimanding unfairly or by picking on a particular pupil, threatens to topple the whole delicate edifice of unspoken mutual expectations on which classroom order rests.

Andrew Pollard, a former head teacher and researcher in primary schools, emphasises the crucial importance of such implicit negotiations:

> The working consensus represents a mutual agreement to respect the dignity and fundamental interests of the other party. As such it is produced by creative and interactive responses to the structural position which teachers and pupils face in their classrooms ... these responses themselves create a micro social structure and context to which individuals have to relate as they act (Pollard, 1985, p. 171).

As Pollard illustrates, what makes a working consensus viable is its relative flexibility: its ability to tolerate minor infringements of official rules, provided they do not go too far. In early dealings with each other, teacher and pupils come to establish a negotiated collective position, in which, without it ever being put into words, each knows more or less what to expect from the other.

An instance that Pollard offers of this working consensus concerns a particular teacher, Mr Harman, at a first school:

> Within Mr Harman's classroom many of the rules were open to negotiation, particularly in circumstances where it was defined as reasonable, or in keeping with the teacher's aims to modify them ... The degree of flexibility varied with Mr Harman's mood and immediate aims, and the children seemed able to sense and detect when rules were non-negotiable ... Mr Harman expects children to come

in when their coats are off, but does not mind delay provided children are in for register and don't hold up administration (Pollard, 1985, p. 165).

As Pollard insists, 'classroom order can endure only if it is based on offering a child fairness and dignity'. By means of the working consensus they establish in their classrooms, many teachers mediate the absolute authority with which institutional structures invest them, and make a space for genuinely human dealings with the young people in their charge.

Nor are such efforts a matter for individual teachers alone. Through whole-school policies, and the shared ethos from which they proceed, institutions themselves can sometimes act to overcome, at least in part, their built-in bureaucratic impersonality. A classic study by Michael Rutter, Peter Mortimore and colleagues (1979) has shown that when this happens, it confers educational as well as social benefits. In a comparison of the relative effectiveness of fifty London primary schools, these researchers found that the more effective schools were characterised by a 'positive school climate'. Pupils felt generally happy and cared for; there was a sense of general enjoyment. These features were associated with teachers who made time for plenty of informal contact with the children. Such teachers organised frequent trips and outings, and arranged after-school and lunch-time clubs. Rather than eating at separate tables, they sat with pupils at lunch, and engaged in non-school chat. In all these ways, such schools had evidently succeeded in moderating the formal and authoritarian nature of institutions and making room for essentially human dealings between the adults and children there.

A recent and particularly dramatic instance of reported institutional transformation is the case of Highfield School (Highfield Junior School, 1997). Over a five-year period this school has, it is claimed, changed from being labelled 'failing' by the Office for Standards in Education, to achieving a 'successful' accolade from the same office. What has happened in the meantime? Gradually, by a process involving all the participants in the school community – from pupils to head teacher, from governors to lunch-time supervisors – the running of the school has become more participative and democratic. Pupils are given responsibility over a wide sphere of school practice. They engage in mediation in disputes, harassment and bullying. As members of a School Council, they hold their own budget. They are involved in interviewing new members of staff. These young people, though still only at the junior stage of education, are treated as capable of sharing a large degree of responsibility for the running of their school.

The outcomes of these changes in institutional practice are said to include improved pupil–pupil and teacher–pupil relationships, and an apparent sense of positive identification with the school on the part of the pupils. Some difficult children have been absorbed into the school community, and there have been no exclusions for the past two years. But the effects have been no less strong where formal achievement levels are concerned: the index on which the success of schooling is conventionally judged. The picture offered in the report is a very rosy one. Its lesson seems clear. Classroom learning proceeds best when pupils are granted personal acknowledgement and respect, and a recognition of their competence, resourcefulness and responsibility.

This kind of experiment in school democracy, apparently so successful in one primary school, would certainly prove a much more difficult undertaking at secondary school. Paradoxically, the scope for flexibility in the running of school business becomes ever narrower as the educational system progresses. Even with the current policing of early learning, via national tests, primary teachers still have more leeway than their colleagues at secondary level. Though considerably more restricted than they were, primary schools retain greater space for personal choice and negotiation with pupils, both in what they teach and in how it is presented. For secondary teachers, on the other hand, the detailed prescriptions of the National Curriculum and the requirements of the GCSE narrowly constrain their sphere of practice.

This is a strange situation. As we generally see things, young people of fifteen or sixteen, relative to five- and six-year-olds, have a far greater capacity to take decisions, to act responsibly, to make their own demands of life. Outside school, our social practices, our social expectations, reflect this assumption. Yet the progression built into our educational institutions is one which, far from enlarging the sphere of personal agency, actually reduces it. The choices at least partly available to pupils in their primary schools – the particular activity, the mode of working – have no place in the lessons of the secondary school. At this level, pupils' classroom activities are closely prescribed, leaving little room for personal negotiation; the option system itself offers only a choice between a limited number of subjects and pre-set ways of working. And the sheer weight of numbers involved, together with the tortuous complexity of the timetabling system, make the routines of school almost immutable: what Ian Craib (1988) has called 'congealed action'.

If this direction is characteristic of the specifically educational aspects of schooling, it is also, perhaps more disastrously, the case where social functioning is concerned. The organisation of the secondary sector makes it difficult for individuals to feel personally recognised, let alone to make a personal impact on the institution itself. School, for most pupils at this level, is an anonymous, impersonal place, with none of the sense of belonging, of ownership, that junior school pupils sometimes feel.

Among the pupils who talked to Jean Rudduck and her colleagues, these features were clearly salient. Transition to secondary school has meant moving from a homely, supportive world to one that is distant and impersonal. Where the school community had been small, with staff who knew pupils and each other, and had at least some contact with parents, young people now face vast numbers, constantly changing groups and brief, strictly academic contacts with teachers. Where school work had previously been interconnected, learning is now separate and compartmentalised.

From these young people's accounts, it can be seen that their anticipations of the 'big school' they now attend were fraught with anxiety. They feared being lost in a huge, confusing building, amongst crowds of unknown people, being bullied by bigger children, impossibly difficult work, overwhelming amounts of homework. Above all, they worried about showing themselves up: being foolish before the audience of their peers.

For many pupils, anxieties such as these are intensified by the comments of others. Lesley Measor and Peter Woods (1984) who made an intensive study of secondary transition, refer to a primary teacher who was apt to tell her pupils, 'You won't get away with work like this there.' More deliberately undermining are the exaggerated stories children sometimes tell each other. These 'pupil myths' retail with relish the dissection of live rats, or the initiation of newcomers by heads thrust down into toilet bowls. Worst-case scenarios such as these are of course rapidly dispelled once children start at secondary school, but, as Measor and Woods discovered, transfer seldom brings happiness. For the young people in their study, progression to secondary level is associated with a decline, both in achievement and in general satisfaction. It is at this level of schooling that disaffection is apt to start.

Additional pressures derive from the selection procedures now introduced by many secondary schools: an eleven-plus system in all but name, though without its public and standardised character. The current market-place philosophy, with its associated league tables of achievement, necessarily puts a premium on pupils' levels of academic attainment. This means that parents, anxious for their children to attend one of the 'better' schools, must try somehow to prepare them for the school's selective tests. Since much of the work required by these tests is not covered in the primary National Curriculum, those parents who can afford it are obliged to engage private tutors. This kind of coaching is highly intensive; different schools use different tests. The situation is typically one of trauma for both children and their parents. And of course it places at a gross disadvantage the many families who lack the social and financial resources needed for such private arrangements.

If the humanising of schools is generally more difficult in the secondary sector, nevertheless many teachers and local authorities have made strenuous efforts to ease the experience of transition. Middle schools, where these have been established, help to bridge different ways of working and to mark out a new pupil status. Greater co-ordination between teaching staff in secondary schools and their feeder primaries have allowed both formal and informal liaison. Induction programmes are now common, with user-friendly welcome booklets, and visits, perhaps including social events attended by older pupils. All these things do of course form part of the general self-marketing in which head teachers are perforce engaged. However, this does not detract from the human contact that they offer, and without which the arrival at a totally new institution can itself be so traumatic.

The currency now in use in the evaluation of educational institutions is that of school effectiveness. 'Effective' primary schools, it is argued, achieve set standards of literacy and numeracy. 'Effective' secondary schools produce a high percentage of respectable grades in GCSE. Following research on 'high' and 'low' achieving schools, a number of general improvement strategies have been identified. These presuppose an essential comparability across different institutions: schools are viewed as a series of replicated arenas tailored to the acquisition of educational attainment. Yet, as is evident to any pupil, parent or teacher, different schools are very different places. They vary in their social and political cultures, in their aspirations, in the lifestyles of their members. Basic to this heterogeneity is social class: a factor that, at least by the secondary stage, divides pupils as much as it divides their elders in adult society.

In contrast with the intake of most primary schools, the pupil populations of secondary schools are currently, and increasingly, socially differentiated. This makes for widely diverse educational cultures. In such a situation, generalisations about school effectiveness can have little meaning. This is evident from a recent study carried out by Sally Brown and her colleagues (1996). In their examination of four secondary schools, these researchers found that the factor of social class held a governing influence over institutional realities. In one school, there was a predominance of pupils from middle-class backgrounds, who brought a positive school orientation: a confidence towards school learning and a strong motivation to achieve. Here, the majority of less able and less advantaged pupils benefited from the close attention of support staff and from the cultural resources of their peers.

In another school, however, whose intake was largely working class, the situation could scarcely have been more different. The self-esteem of these young people was unrelated to school achievement; and there was generally little motivation towards school learning. Support staff were greatly outnumbered by pupils with learning difficulties. Teaching aims in this school, as these researchers insist, were necessarily very unlike those that applied in its more privileged counterpart.

Such diversity, as Brown suggests, must put a question mark over generalisations about school 'effectiveness'. For teachers struggling to work with pupils who see little point in classroom learning, the current rhetoric can carry little weight: 'Telling them that effective schools are associated with strong and competent leadership, particular patterns of punishment and reward systems, management structures, committed staff with high expectations and standards, and so on, is likely to be greeted with "That's all very well, but somewhat distant from what faces me as a teacher"' (Brown et al., 1996, p. 88).

By the secondary stage, schools represent highly distinctive human contexts. What works in one will not work in another. Yet initiatives to turn round 'ineffective' schools have been typically based on supposedly universal, context-free principles of improvement. These emphasise such factors as strong administrative leadership, the generation of higher teacher expectations, the acquisition of basic skills, and the constant monitoring of pupils' performance. While probably few people would question these goals as defined in abstract, the actual implementation of strategies for change is another matter. As John Gray and Brian Wilcox (1996) argue in a discussion of this question, these strategies presuppose a general consensus as to the current ineffectiveness of a school, and an enthusiastic commitment to working for change. Yet for teaching staff in many schools labelled in this way, there is no such consensus and no such commitment. In consequence, challenges to established practices may be met with resistance and a closing of ranks.

Efforts at school improvement are, in these writers' words, 'perched on the back of staff whose goodwill is, almost certainly, stretched already'. Without the personal endorsement, the genuine conviction of the teachers involved, such efforts are doomed to fail. It is only when teaching staff themselves share a sense of new possibilities and a sense of personally owning the initiatives to be taken, that there is hope of institutional transformation. For such change involves much more than the modification of particular practices; it implicates the whole prevailing culture and ethos of the school. And these are things that belong to teachers and to pupils, both of whom need to be actively involved in any attempt at improvement. Bottom-up initiatives in schools have been generally far more successful than those imposed from above. This is exemplified in one such project recently launched by the Local Educational Authority of Hammersmith and Fulham (Stoll, Myers and Harrington, 1994). Its aims are defined as 'laying the foundations for raising student levels of attainment, achievement and morale' within eight secondary schools within the borough. The project is designed to ensure that ownership of initiative is in the hands of staff and pupils. The work is essentially implemented by teaching staff working closely together: sharing ideas about school culture, and acting as 'critical friends' in each other's classrooms. These strategies do not exclude the concerns of pupils. Through teacher–pupil negotiation, a mentoring system is established to help with literacy skills. And for those taking national exams, course work clinics are set up outside schooltime.

The overall success of this scheme, entitled 'Schools Make a Difference', surely relates to its embeddedness within the particular, and different, school contexts in which it is carried out. Far from trying to impose improvement from outside, the project gives control of change strategies to the people whose practices they affect. Institutional improvement is seen as a highly individualised process. This is born out of the recognition that the kinds of change appropriate and possible are not a product of universally applicable principles, but are very particular to context. Surely this has implications for the way we should view the possibilities for institutional change. In the words of Andy Hargreaves, 'Faith in generalised and scientifically known principles of school effectiveness has begun to be superseded by commitments to more ongoing, provisional and contextually sensitive processes of school improvement' (1994, p. 54).

4

Children as Thinkers

If our schooling system typically ignores the social and personal experience of its pupils, that is because its essential agenda is an intellectual one. Children go to school, we assume, to develop their cognitive abilities: to come, through their learning of the curriculum, to a higher level of mental competence. This development takes place, we generally believe, through a careful tailoring of formal school learning to the child's current level of cognitive functioning. For the young have built-in tendencies to mature, and alongside the natural increments in height and strength to adult scale, there is a similar gradual progression in the capacity to think and understand.

The maturation process that is thought to govern intellectual growth represents an unfolding of innate capacities. Like physical development, it is a movement upwards, towards an end point: that of adulthood, maturity. As will be suggested presently, the characterisation of adult intellectual functioning that this entails is very much open to challenge, but the assumption of initial incompetence may perhaps be no less questionable.

Little children starting school cannot, it seems, manage anything but the simplest educational curriculum. In nursery schools and reception classes, furnishings are typically uninstitutional: homely, informal, cosy. The activities offered are essentially playlike, with props intended as extensions of already familiar toys and materials. In this context, teachers work to develop children's understanding through the elicitation of concepts referring to immediate experience. Their questions of their young charges relate to the here and now: to the sensory qualities of play materials, for instance, or to the effects of certain kinds of action. Prime among such interrogations, as part of the educationally prized domain of mathematics, are questions about numerical and relational properties.

Valerie Walkerdine (1988), a critic of developmental psychology, describes her own experiment with a number of nursery school children. This involves a seriation task: ordering three bears of ascending size. Here is an extract from her testing of one child:

> V. W.: 'Which one's the daddy bear?'
> Child points to biggest bear.
> V. W.: 'Which one's the mummy bear?
> Child points to middle bear.
> V. W.: 'Which one's the baby bear?'
> Child points to smallest bear.
> V. W.: 'Is the daddy bear bigger than the mummy bear?'
> Child shakes his head.

As Walkerdine describes, responses such as these are common with young children, suggesting that they do not yet understand the meaning of relational terms. It is assumed

that the comparative terms 'bigger' and 'smaller' are developmentally more complex than the more directly experienced
'big' and 'little'. To Walkerdine, however, the matter is far
more complicated.

Walkerdine's analysis locates children's understanding of
size relations not within the realm of abstract mathematics,
but in the context of family relations:

> Little is a term which has important and multiple signifi-
> cations in the lives of young children, in which it is used
> not indiscriminately, but to denote a specific set of relation-
> ships ... For example, the terms 'baby', 'tiny' and 'little'
> are used synonymously, as are 'big' and 'mummy'. It is
> important that 'big' and 'daddy' are not used cotermi-
> nously. This gives a firm basis for suggesting that there is
> a problem about the use of 'mummy' as the 'middle' term,
> since if mummy is read as big it could prove difficult for
> some children to make the leap to using the term 'middle
> sized' for designating her position. In several exchanges
> 'mummy' and 'baby' or 'big'/'baby', 'little'/'mummy' are
> used as contrastive pairs ... 'baby' and 'mummy' form a
> contrastive pair in which size, status and power are coter-
> minous (Walkerdine, 1988, pp. 65–6).

To many writers about children's development, this
example would serve only to prove their own case: that
young children are too embedded in their own practical
realities to be capable of grasping the concepts on which real
thought depends. Intellectual development, so runs the argument, proceeds from concrete to abstract: from a dependence
on the here and now, to an understanding of categories and
principles that transcend the immediacy of experience.

The assumption that cognitive development proceeds from
concrete to abstract is a very basic one. It seems self-evident

that understandings embedded within practicalities are necessarily more primitive than ideas that are independent of any particular content. To be able to deal with concepts as such, mentally to manipulate purely formal categories and principles: this appears to represent a very high order of intellectual functioning. Such an assumption is fundamental to the progression of schooling. While the education of little children takes a form that is active, sensory and physical, primary schooling becomes ever less tied to first-hand practical experience, initially through the acquisition of literacy and numeracy. This progression continues at secondary level, where curriculum content becomes ever more formal, and the subjects with the highest status are the most abstract ones of maths and science.

If concrete forms of thinking seem to be more rudimentary than abstract ones, this is because they apparently tie the thinker to particular circumstances; they restrict consideration to the viewpoint of the current situation. The classic example of this argument is represented by one of the experiments devised by Jean Piaget, the eminent Swiss theorist whose formulations of children's cognitive development have been massively influential in education. In his test of the understanding of perspective, the child is asked to look at a model of three mountains, and then to match a series of pictures, taken from various angles, with particular nominated points of observation. As Piaget found, children of five and six are typically unable to perform this task correctly. In his formulation, their essentially concrete way of thinking fixes them immovably within their own viewpoint, so that they cannot properly envisage another.

More recently, a number of people have challenged Piaget's argument. Margaret Donaldson (1978), a Scottish psychologist, was among the first to do so in an ingenious reworking of Piaget's original experiment. Instead of simply looking at pictures of the mountain, the child is asked to put a small doll somewhere in the model where it can hide from two doll-policemen, placed at different positions there. Given this task, five- and six-year-olds are much more likely to succeed. It seems that when the problem is posed in terms of characters and activities that children can interpret, they are markedly less egocentric in their thinking, and can move away, imaginatively, from their own immediate viewpoint. As Donaldson puts it, they can deal with questions that make human sense.

This example suggests that, paradoxically, tasks that come embedded in day-to-day practical experience elicit a higher order of thinking than those that are posed in purely abstract terms, free of any particular human content. This conclusion is certainly borne out by a study of nursery school children conducted some years ago by Barbara Tizard and Martin Hughes (1984). These London-based researchers studied thirty four-year-old girls, making detailed comparisons of their talk in conversations at home and with their nursery school teachers. They did this through small microphones sewn into the children's clothes. What this study showed, to a startling extent, was the cognitive superiority of 'home talk' over that of school.

Chatting with their mothers at home, these little girls constantly show a lively intellectual curiosity. Struggling to understand a new word or idea, or fit new information into what they already know, they emerge, in their researchers' words, as 'persistently questioning, puzzling minds'. Yet in the context of nursery school, they are characteristically subdued and passive. Exchanges with teachers are low-key and flat, with none of the spontaneity or the complexity of their conversations at home. Their talk here tends to be monosyllabic and short-lived, consisting of minimal responses to their teachers' questions.

These findings are, on the face of it, very surprising. Nursery schools, after all, are designed to be educational: to stimulate children's intellectual curiosity, to develop their understanding. Unlike those of mothers, teachers' purposes are exclusively educational. Not having to make room for children amidst multiple family and domestic responsibilities, they can give undivided attention to their charges. Yet somehow this setting fails to elicit the mental liveliness so characteristic of young children's functioning at home.

The impetus to intellectual development, as most teachers would argue, is enquiry. It is through the questions that we put to the world that we construct our understanding of it. And the little girls in this study do persistently, urgently ask questions – of their mothers. In their nursery school setting, however, they apparently find nothing to ask of their teachers; instead, it is their teachers who question them. The intellectual level of the two sorts of exchanges is strikingly different, for while, in their own questioning, these girls launch into long, often elaborate, conversational exchanges, their teachers' questioning typically falls flat.

The interrogations of young children, and those of their teachers, are of course of a very different order. As they chat with their mothers – over domestic chores, a meal, the changing or feeding of the baby – these small girls are characteristically preoccupied with some feature of their everyday lives. Family relationships, household affairs, the social world they live in and know about: these are the spheres to which questions are addressed; and as located within their own and their mothers' daily lives, these questions presuppose a shared experience. What is in common between questioner and respondent covers wide spans of time and space: many places known to both, a shared past and present, and a lively anticipation of a shared future.

These enquiries are very far from being abstract; they are positively loaded with human content.

The questions that, for their part, nursery teachers put to their charges are necessarily very different. Their enquiries, as Tizard and Hughes describe them, typically centre on children's use of play materials; they ask questions about colour, volume, number or causal relationships. Such interrogations are located in the here and now, rather than referring to other times and places. And, so far from being embedded in the particular contexts, interests and involvements of individual children, they are essentially generalised, abstract and impersonal.

The highest form of thought, we generally suppose, are defined by their rationality. Unencumbered by human particulars, the mind follows the pure logic of universal principles to arrive at clear, unchallengeable conclusions. This is thinking at its most abstract. And as the embodiments of cognitive maturity – the pinnacle to which more primitive thought must aspire – it is supposedly adults who characteristically engage in this kind of thought.

But this assumption, though it is implicit in our conventional wisdom, cannot stand serious consideration. Disputes between adults and children are probably far less often resolved by reasoning than by the simple weight of authority: 'because I say so'. The sheer irrationality that is all too evident in human affairs, whether local, national or international, suggests that men and women seldom base their judgements on reasoning alone. Far from arising from the logic of distinterested general principles, our social agency is characteristically governed by partiality and self-interest. Important political decisions are made on the basis of personalities rather than policies. Dealings with 'other' human groups are typically swayed by primitive prejudices impervious to contrary evidence. Nor do self-interested forms of action always follow their own logic, as witness the massive self-inflicted injuries involved in many relationship breakups, or civil wars.

Rationality, it is clear, does not constitute the guiding principle in the everyday thinking of adult men and women. But reasoning, as such, may in any case not represent the best criterion for evaluating human thought. That is the position taken by Valerie Walkerdine, who sets out to challenge the traditional supremacy of this feature. Rationality, she argues, is based on an illusion, on wishful thinking. Rational thinking seems to offer us total mastery: the regulation of our lives and our selves in an ordered, predictable, controllable world. But human realities are not like that. Fraught with uncertainties, subject to untameable forces, both outside and within ourselves, the world we live in can never be encompased within the neat and tidy formulations of pure logic.

Something of Walkerdine's case is surely acknowledged in our best social institutions. The legal system, for example, recognises that human affairs cannot simply be subjected to the application of an a priori logic. Right and wrong are not to be judged by a set of universal principles, divorced from the particulars of human context. Circumstances *do* alter cases. The delicate judgments that must be made about crime and punishment are, as many judges and juries have discovered, far more difficult, far more complex, than the simple application of a logical syllogism.

It seems that in the spheres of life that possess the greatest human significance, a kind of thinking is called for that is very different from abstract rationality. In the law courts, where nothing less than life and death is at stake, we rely not on principles of human particulars, but on the deeply thoughtful weighing and consideration of unique local circumstances: material conditions, character and competence, human purposes and motives, social norms and expectations.

The legal system demands, if it does not always elicit, a high level of mental functioning. Decisions are not to be lightly or arbitrarily arrived at. Thinking must engage with the actual present, rather than being biased by pre-judgments. A multitude of factors must be assimilated, taken into account, weighed one against another. This process is rarely easy; 'evidence' is typically ambiguous and contradic-tory. But it is the only means we have in our struggle towards the truth: a truth that is humanly meaningful. If few of us achieve the capacity to think like this, except occasionally, nevertheless the development of such a capacity must repre-sent a worthy goal.

In considering cognitive development, we need perhaps to reverse our traditional assumptions about the most advanced, as against the most rudimentary, forms of thought. The idea that intellectual progression follows a journey from concrete to abstract no longer seems a tenable one. Faced with a problem in perspective, as Donaldson shows, six-year-olds are more, not less, effective when the problem is embedded in humanly meaningful particulars. As evidenced by the findings of Tizard and Hughes, young children exhibit a livelier and more profound involvement in thinking about their local, personal contexts than in considering the abstract properties of objects to which teachers draw their attention. And in adult social institutions where the most sustained, the most explicit, the most complex forms of thinking are called for, local particulars, so far from being deemed irrelevant, are given weighty consideration.

These concerns have implications both for the curriculum of schooling, and for the modes in which young people's thinking may need to be couched. A later chapter will argue for a different perspective on contexted and acontextual aspects of the school curriculum, and for the possibilities of narrative forms of learning and thinking as embodying vital human content.

Theoretical discussion of thinking typically locates it within the dimensions of abstractness and rationality. However, very different terms are offered by Michael Billig, a psychologist who has devoted many years to the close study of human thought. In his book *Arguing and Thinking* (1987), Billig depicts thinking as an essentially social process, in which argumentation has pride of place.

If thinking is a matter of following the rules of reason, then there is always a guaranteed end point: a right answer. But to Billig, there is no such thing as absolute correctness; the criterion can only be that of consensual agreement. Human thought is not a solitary enterprise; it exists within a social, an interpersonal, context. It is through dialogue with others that we develop our intellectual capacity: our ability to consider issues, to pose questions, to take moral positions; and in such dialogue, it is controversy, challenge and argument that constitute the essential dynamic.

Children, suggests Billig, develop intellectually through early quarrels. Wanting to secure or maintain some resource against another's wishes, they are forced to justify themselves: to find reasons for the stance they are taking, to point out exceptional circumstances. The personal investment of young people in certain outcomes within their personal lives turns their everyday conversations into occasions for advocacy. In order to defend their own position, they must explain apparent discrepancies or articulate qualifications to a rule. The energy and imagination that their own involvement gives these conversations is, Billig argues, developmentally very important. For in private thinking, it is this experience of public argument that enables our own inner argumentative discourse: our exploration and comparison of alternative possibilities.

Not all arguments, as Billig concedes, are so developmentally fertile. Many debates are far from open. Opponents may be speaking from entrenched positions, adopting rude and aggressive tactics to browbeat each other, using conversation competitively – not to exchange viewpoints, but merely to score points. Such arguments do little to advance the development of the conversational skills so vital to thinking. For this depends on the absence of a rigid stance. Proper argument means listening. Participants must accept another's point of view, however, alien, as at least worthy of consideration. There has to be a preparedness to be persuaded: a willingness to change one's mind in the course of conversation. This itself can be uncomfortable, not just because of possible loss of face, but also because it necessarily entails a period of indecision, of provisionality.

One feature that must militate against good argumentation is inequality between participants; and it is here that institutionalised schooling makes for difficulty. If school learning is to help pupils develop intellectually, it needs to provide opportunities for argumentative kinds of talk. Ideally, and naturally, argument flourishes between equal participants. But classroom learning seldom entails discussions between pupils themselves, although, as will be illustrated later, some teachers do manage to make room for this kind of engagement. To an overwhelming extent, however, school talk takes place between teachers and pupils; and the conventional teacher–pupil relation is, as the previous chapter argued, one of domination–subordination. Where conversational authority is heavily invested in one side of the dialogue, communication can hardly be unconstrained. Good argument demands spontaneity, imagination, creative daring; this is impossible when the imbalance of power effectively forestalls challenge and the offering of contrary positions.

Classroom discourse, in its traditional form, represents almost everything that is inimical to the development of the kind of argument that Billig advocates. Though the conversation is nominally two-sided, nevertheless particpation on the part of pupils is typically perfunctory and ritualistic. Questions, so far from taking the debate further, are likely to be hollow. Teachers, as interrogators, already know the answer to their question, as pupils are perfectly aware. Their enquiries are themselves often somewhat mechanical; neither side has a burning personal interest in the response. If pupils themselves put questions, these are very far from being challenges to teachers' positions. For it is hardly possible for learners to challenge their official mentors to provide evidence for their claims, or justify the importance of what they offer in the classroom. Instead, these questions merely represent a checking-out of how to follow the 'party line'.

Equally inhibiting for the fostering of classroom argument are the assumptions that lie behind the traditional curriculum of schooling. Received wisdom has it that the knowledge offered children in school classrooms is absolute and for all time. In this, there is no room for challenge, for allowing that there are always other ways of viewing things, that human truths are relative, and established by a changing social consensus. The conventional philosophy of knowledge, as built into much of the schooling system, acts to discourage serious argument, and to make instead for what Billig dubs 'reverent repetition'. But this position towards knowledge, so detrimental to the development of thinking, is one that many people have begun to challenge. The educational implications of this challenge, and the ways in which some teachers and researchers are following these through in classroom work, will be described later in the book.

5

Marking Competence

Ours has been described as a credentialist society: a society that continually breeds more and more qualifications of less and less worth. Certainly one of the most oppressive features of school life, in the experience of many young people and many parents, is the endless round of testing. On top of the tests through which teachers must regularly check their own classroom work, come national tests, the Standard Assessment Tests. At seven, eleven and fourteen, every pupil must undergo these trials, before the ultimate test at sixteen: the General Certificate of Secondary Education. These assessments cannot be lightly dismissed; their outcome carries fateful destinies.

The rationale for all this measuring activity is regularly rehearsed. Public accountability, so goes the rhetoric, demands regular monitoring of educational standards, to ensure that every school is 'performing' adequately. In line with market principles, national test results are publicly presented to parents, as consumers, in the form of league tables. Supposedly enlarging parental choice, these tables only create a rush for limited places at the 'better' schools, inevitably leading to disappointment for many parents.

The competence-marking built into the school regime is burdensome – not just for pupils, but for teachers too. National tests entail huge amounts of extra, essentially bureaucratic work, on top of already heavy loads: preparation, administration, marking. In themselves, they often add little to teaching concerns. Nationwide applicablity demands a generalised content that takes no account of the particular directions and interests involved in individual classroom work. The need to ensure a marking system that is simple and watertight tends to mean a format of short, timed, written tasks, performed in controlled conditions. This is quite unlike the interactive and multi-modal approach through which many teachers prefer to make their own assessments. Increasingly, such tests have come to focus on closed questions, sometimes even involving multiple choice.

Though necessarily time-consuming, such assessments are often seen by teachers as irrelevant to learning. As one interviewee remarks to Peter Woods, 'It's not for the children's benefit . . . it doesn't enhance the children's learning . . . I don't think anybody would mind so much spending all this time if you really felt the children's learning was being enhanced' (Woods, 1996, p. 45). The capacities tested by formats such as these are inevitably a long way from the kind of thinking discussed in the previous chapter. The paper and pencil tasks that represent the substance of these tests are scarcely capable of eliciting the ability to consider complex ideational material, to follow through lines of implication, to think flexibly, to exercise judgement. Indeed, the emphasis on product rather than process necessarily entails individualised testing, and precludes the oral modes and group settings that can provide the opportunity for the display of thought-in-action.

When teachers devise their own, informal, purpose-built forms of educational assessment, they use these as checks on teaching: sampling their pupils' level of understanding in order to plan the next stage of classroom work. Their aim is essentially future-directed. These assessments are dynamic rather than static. They are intended not to fix particular pupils at differential points on a pre-existing scale, but rather to diagnose strengths and weaknessness, at group as well as individual level, as a guide to the appropriate direction of the next phase of classroom learning. As such, they are, in current phraseology, not summative, but formative.

A feature of teachers' own forms of attainment testing is that their content, unlike that of national tests, is tailored to their own particular curriculum, modes of learning, and specific pupil group. Some experimental forms of assessment have taken this logic still further, in relating uniquely to individual pupils. Here, assessment rests not on some external criterion of generalised, age-related achievement, but on comparison with that particular pupil's previous level of achievement. In these self-related – rather then normative – forms of testing, the performance of learners is compared with their own previous performance. This is a definition of attainment in terms of the progress actually made by individual learners. The approach is one that aims not merely to measure learning, but to promote it.

Elizabeth Adams and Tyrrell Burgess (1992) have together pioneered the use in schools of two such assessment formats: records of achievement and personal portfolios. Records of achievement document what young people themselves judge to be the best pieces of work they have done over the past year. Such work may extend beyond classroom activities, to include out-of-school achievements. However, all these forms of attainment have to be accredited by others: teachers, external bodies, or those considered expert in the particular field concerned.

Personal portfolios, which also entail inventories of personal accomplishment, require young people not merely to record attainments, but to reflect on the significance of each for further learning, and to include such reflections within the account offered. This aspect gives pupils much greater responsibility than is usual for managing and evaluating their own learning. As Adams and Burgess argue, many school leavers regret, often bitterly, the lack of opportunities to attend to areas and modes of learning that seem in retrospect to have been crucial in their own educational failure: 'In most schools, individual students are not called upon to reflect on their work, to recognise their own abilities, or to identify those weaknesses which could reduce their chances of fulfilling their own purposes' (Adams and Burgess, 1992, p. 118).

In involving young people in making their own judgements of personal strengths and weaknesses, these kinds of assessment offer a radical departure from traditional forms. This feature might be imagined to lead to exaggerated claims and general self-aggrandisement, but Adams and Burgess have found that, if anything, pupils tend to be overly self-critical in evaluating their own achievements. Certainly the exercise is one that is taken seriously, quite unlike conventional educational assessments, which are typically experienced as an unwanted and threatening imposition.

For a time during the 1980s, before the government tightened its grip still further on the educational system, records of achievement were adopted in a number of primary schools, and a few secondary ones. Some secondary schools also tried out the more ambitious statements of learning progress entailed in personal portfolios. But the generous and affirmative spirit that inspires these kinds of assessment does not sit easily with the market philosophy presently dominant. Far from aiming to celebrate and develop the positive achievement of every school pupil, current approaches set out to classify young people into winners and losers. The technologies of measurement in general use are founded on the assumption that educational ability is distributed over a range, on which as many children will fall below the average as the numbers of those above it. Marking incompetence, from this viewpoint, is as important as recording success.

Caroline Gipps (Gipps and Murphy, 1994), an authority on educational assessment, argues that this assumption all too easily becomes a self-fulfilling prophecy; 'achievement' depends on how it is assessed. When, as she puts it, evaluation aims to sentence rather then to help pupils, there will be many consignments to the category of failure. And just as the accolade of success confers a confident sense of personal capacity, so children labelled failures can acquire an unshakeable conviction of their own stupidity.

An experiment by Robert Hartley (1986), entitled 'Imagine You're Clever', provides a startling illustration of this situation. Hartley worked with children aged seven and eight from disadvantaged backgrounds. All were judged to be of low ability by their primary school teachers, who had very limited expectations of their future educational progress. In his experiment, Hartley worked with a test known as the Matching Familiar Figures Test. It involves a task often featured in children's comics: matching a figure with one of a series of slightly different alternatives. Responses are marked on a scale of impulsiveness-versus-reflectiveness. Impulsiveness is, it is claimed, statistically associated with a low level of intelligence.

In his experiment, Hartley invites his subjects to perform the test twice. After doing it in the usual way, he asks them to do it again, but this time to imagine that they are someone who is 'very, very clever'. The two performances are quite different. When acting as 'themselves', the children perform impulsively, responding to each task quickly, with many inaccuracies. Yet when 'being someone clever', they approach the test cautiously, and deliberately, with a marked concern for accuracy. Unlike their previous responses, the responses they make in this unfamiliar role score at the 'reflective' end of the scale.

For traditional ways of thinking about competence, this outcome seems almost incomprehensible. We generally suppose individual differences in ability to be an innate property of people, as fixed and unalterable as the colour of our eyes. Yet children, in playfully exchanging personal identities, can, apparently at will, perform at levels of competence assumed to be beyond them. This can only mean that what we call intellectual ability, so far from being an inborn set of limits, is at least in part a product of the kinds of people we are, and are seen to be.

The children in Hartley's study came from working-class homes, associated with material and cultural disadvantage. This is hardly surprising. Social disadvantage is characteristic of the groups typically defined as lacking cognitive ability and concomitant educational potential. Among these groups, working-class and African–Caribbean children predominate.

Schools, it is said, cannot compensate for society. Our social order is marked by inequalities: of power, status, resources of every kind; and as institutions that serve the status quo, schools cannot but act to reproduce these inequalities. Functioning as it does to grade and classify young people, our educational system confers differentiated judgements of competence upon its pupils, with inevitable consequences for their future life chances. Many of those who work in schools strive to mitigate this function: to champion the disadvantaged, to create classrooms that are places of equality for all. It is sometimes possible, as suggested earlier in this book, to moderate many of the institutional features that particularly oppress certain groups of pupils. But this is never easy nor complete; the system has in-built biases that favour white middle-class pupils over those who are black and working class, and, despite the current rise in female achievement, has generally set a higher value on boys than on girls.

If the schooling system differentially privileges pupils according to their race, class and gender, this is scarcely surprising. Major social institutions reflect the norms, values and vital interests of dominant groups. In our own society, as few people would now deny, it is white middle-class men who charcteristically occupy positions of power. This is also generally the case in schools. At primary level, despite the predominance of women teachers, disproportionate numbers of men hold headships. In the higher-status world of secondary education, male heads greatly outnumber female ones, just as men are over-represented as heads of department, particularly in high-status subjects such as maths and science. When it comes to ancillary staff, male posts such as caretaker have higher standing, and are better paid, than the prototypically female jobs of cleaner or dinner lady.

It is not only in literal terms, however, that the schooling system carries its differential treatment. As an institution, it embodies dominant cultural forms. Its regime, its agenda, its modes of conduct are tailored to a particular rather than a universal lifestyle. Its most valued product, attainment in traditionally academic subjects, fits pupils for an adult career typically dominated by white middle-class men.

Within this system, teachers are necessarily instrumental. This is not to say that as a group the teaching profession endorses the unequal outcomes of most formal education. Many of those involved are deeply committed to social equality, and use their work, as far as they can, to enhance it. But there are profoundly entrenched biases within the institutions of schooling, and there is active promotion of competition and hierarchy by government and educational pressure groups. In so far as they are obliged to serve the grading function of schooling, teachers inevitably play their part in the allocation of privilege and disadvantage.

The institution of schooling requires teachers to make differential judgements of pupils' educational competence. It is, perhaps, only to be expected that those who fit effortlessly into the modes and demands of formal schooling will be seen as more naturally able than those who seem not to grasp their importance, or who struggle actively against them.

An early, highly influential case study illustrates how this can happen. The school studied by Rachel Sharp and Tony Green (1975) was a 'progressive' primary school, with an emphasis on discovery methods of learning. Teachers based their work with children on evidence of 'readiness'; pupils were offered new learning opportunities only when they showed signs of having reached the appropriate level of understanding. In this teaching context, some pupils were judged as markedly more mature, cognitively, than others. The activities and behaviour of working-class children tended consistently to be seen as lacking intellectual maturity. Their teachers attributed this apparently poor level of development to deprivation through unstimulating homes, which were effectively pathologised.

As these researchers argue, the definition of developmental level, and its imagined indications, involve judgements that are loaded with social class values. They presuppose forms of behaviour that are standard in middle-class homes, but atypical, or even proscribed, among working-class families. Play, for instance, so important an activity for these kinds of judgements, is likely to mean something very different in an affluent, well-resourced and spacious household, than in an impoverished, crowded home in an unsafe neighbourhood. 'Initiative', 'creativeness', 'adventurousness', 'spontaneity':

these qualities, favoured by a progressive educational ethos, presuppose a well-resourced family background characteristic of middle- rather than working-class groups.

Progressive kinds of schooling, prominent at primary level during the 1970s, were based on an explicit commitment to social and educational equality. Yet even here, built-in inequalities proved apparently impossible to eradicate: 'Where the teachers display a moral concern that every child matters, in practice there is a subtle process of sponsorship . . . where opportunity is offered to some and closed off to others' (Sharp and Green, 1975, p. 218). With its emphasis on children's play, this approach to education foregrounds personal and social aspects of behaviour. But such features also enter, in a multitude of subtle ways, into judgements about competences made, ostensibly, on a purely cognitive basis.

Classroom discourse is fundamental in the relations between teachers and their pupils. Each can know the other only through their mutual talk, and different groups of young people speak differently. In the low educational potential that is typically accorded to black pupils, language is heavily implicated. The apparent inadequacy of such pupils, as speakers, has given rise to a large body of research. The outcomes of early work of this kind seemed generally to confirm the assumption that black children are incapable of more than rudimentary forms of language. When formally tested, it was found, they characteristically use simple, rather than elaborate, sentence structures, suggesting some kind of linguistic impoverishment.

This conclusion, however, has been strongly contested. William Labov (1969), an American sociologist, was one of the first voices to challenge the assumption of deficit. Labov bases his case on observation of young black people talking together in their own communities. As against their typically stilted, even monosyllabic responses to questioning by white middle-class academics in laboratory settings, children and adolescents, on their own territory, talk rationally and wittily, showing themselves to be highly articulate, with a command of complex linguistic forms, and a capacity for lively argument and debate.

As Labov insists, it is factors within the social and institutional contexts of talk that make for such striking differences. In test situations, children cannot but be aware that they are under judgement from white middle-class representatives of authority. What can be said in this context is quite unlike the linguistic possibilities of relaxed and friendly discourse with one's peers.

Yet, despite evidence such as this, the characterisation of black pupils continues to portray them as educationally incompetent; and language, it seems, is still significant in this perception. Though the linguistic situation is not quite the same as the one that prevailed in the 1960s and 1970s, nevertheless there remain distinctive features of black language that exercise an influence on the generally negative evaluations made by teachers. Among these, the use of creole forms, which are beyond most teachers' comprehension, can prove alienating – as, of course, is sometimes intended.

The world of school, as an essentially white middle-class world, carries built-in disadvantages for black and working-class children; and these disadvantages are mediated, however unwillingly, by teachers themselves. For teachers' own personal experience and social situation are likely to lie much closer to those of white middle-class pupils than to other pupil groups.

The relationship between teachers and their pupils is the focus of an unpublished study by Mary Baur (1981). Baur worked with a number of primary school teachers and their classroom groups, to elicit how they perceived themselves and each other. She found that those children that their teachers consider to be 'good pupils' typically use the same kinds of description, the same dimensions of meaning, that their teachers use. Children classified by their teachers as educationally incompetent or unwilling, by contrast, use a quite different frame of reference; what rates for them, in evaluating themselves and others, is not what rates as significant for their teachers. Similarity in personal frames of reference may, it seems, foster, and result from, positive judgements of educational competence.

Evaluation of educational ability is a lengthy and complex process, in which not just individual teachers are involved, but a gradually negotiated staff consensus. Particular pupils come to acquire various reputations through the sharing of teacher experiences, perhaps especially in staffroom interchanges. Once crystallised within a known identity, it is hard for a young person to be seen differently. As Hartley's study shows, we all act 'in character'; when 'being themselves', his young subjects behave as their school image suggests they should. And altered behaviour may in any case make little difference. For classroom performance, no matter what form it takes, is likely to be interpreted in terms of established identity: who you are can, in this sense, be more important than what you do.

A striking illustration of what this can mean in schooling judgements concerns the situation of girls. In an ingenious experiment, Margaret Goddard-Spear (1983) gave the same pieces of science writing to a number of teachers to mark; some were told they were the work of male pupils, while for others they were attributed to female pupils. Teachers believing boys had produced the writings marked them significantly higher than teachers who thought they were the work of girls.

The sphere of science, like that of maths, holds particular importance in educational evaluations. These are the most abstract subjects in the school curriculum and as such are generally thought to entail the highest forms of thinking: those of rationality, which, as suggested earlier, supposedly represent the pinnacle of intellectual development. And here, factors to do with gender are generally thought to play a very important part, for, in received wisdom, males and females are characterised very differently. Objectivity, dispassionate, logical thought: these are masculine preserves, in contrast with the emotionality, the reliance on intuition, the intellectual weakness of feminine character. In shorthand, males are believed to think, females to feel.

There is, as Valerie Walkerdine (1988) argues, a strong investment in the intellectual pre-eminence of the masculine world. As part of her consideration of this belief, she has carried out a careful and extensive study of the performance of girls in maths. Like other researchers in this sphere of the curriculum, Walkerdine notes that, despite the stereotype of female incompetence, girls generally do well in this subject – at least at primary level. Yet these outcomes are regularly explained away by their teachers. Such is the conviction that maths is not a girls' subject and that girls are not naturally clever, that even outstanding performance comes to be downgraded.

Female achievement, when it exceeds that of boys, is characterised by the teachers concerned as just the result of hard work and rule-following. Where male pupils are described as 'creative', 'brilliant', and 'having flair', even if often lazy or disruptive, their female counterparts attract no such attributions, being described as mere plodders: 'conscientious' and 'conforming'. Boys are seen as having natural aptitude, while girls have no real understanding, but only follow learned routines. In this way, evidence that runs counter to conventional wisdom comes to be rewritten to support it.

It is precisely on these grounds that many advocates of formal standardised testing base their case. In teachers' assessments, in judgements made informally with their own local contexts, material and pupils, biases, it is argued, can all too easily creep in. Far better to rely on universally applicable and objective tests. The standardised, statistically regulated scoring system incorporated in such measures makes them, in that unkind phrase, 'teacher-proof': impervious to personal prejudices and predilections; and of all such measurements, surely intelligence tests are the fairest. For in tapping pure cognitive ability, independently of achievement, they reveal educational potential, unaffected by the accidents of particular classroom histories.

Yet, as Caroline Gipps (Gipps and Murphy, 1994), a contemporary critic, insists, the apparent objectivity of standardised tests is essentially an illusion. Features that favour certain social groups over others are present right from the beginning. Though the content of intelligence tests may seem neutral – equally familiar, equally comprehensible to any testee – in fact items have necessarily been selected by the test developers, themselves members of a particular social and cultural grouping. Their norms, their values, dictate the domain from which these items are chosen, the mode of response demanded of testees, and the standards in terms of which the correctness of their answers is to be judged. As Gipps puts it, test construction is 'mediated by cultural knowledge'.

However seemingly objective, intelligence testing builds in disadvantages for members of other, non-dominant groups. But because the generally low scores characteristic of such groups accord with social stereotypes, test results tend to be seen as 'true', rather than as an artefact of the test itself. Such assumptions have, over a number of years, come under vigorous criticism. As Gipps remarks, 'The cultural, social and gender group of the test developers is the one which defines what is normal and high status; those who cannot match this are ipso facto inferior, rather than just different' (Gipps and Murphy, 1994, p. 263). The point is made more strongly still by Patricia Broadfoot (1979): 'IQ testing legitimates the perpetuation of class inequalities, through defining scores as objective and scientific ... teaching the doomed majority that their failure was the result of their own inbuilt inadequacy' (Broadfoot, 1979, p. 44).

Yet in the course of its development, the most widely used children's intelligence test was found to have anomalies. When the battery of items making up the test was tried out on a vast sample of children, boys performed at a significantly lower level than girls. This might have been interpreted, like the generally low scores of working-class and black testees, as showing a genuinely poor level of cognitive ability. But since, to the test constructors, boys were 'known' to be the intellectual equals of girls, if not actually superior, such a conclusion was not to be entertained for a moment. Instead, these outcomes were defined as revealing failures in test construction. The items were sent back to the drawing board, and the test was reworked to remove these inequalities.

An opposite logic, as Gipps points out, applies in the case of girls' generally poor showing on certain other, equally 'objective' tests of ability: 'More effort has gone into exploring cognitive deficits in girls to explain their poor performance than into asking whether the reliance on tasks and apparatus associated with upper class white males could possibly have something to do with it' (Gipps and Murphy, 1994, p. 263).

Educational evaluation that does equal justice to every social group is clearly not easily achieved. Current pressures towards competition and hierarchy mean the allocation of many pupils to the category of failure. Focusing assessments on positive achievement and the acknowledgement of success involves battling against the dominant ethos.

The inequalities of our society also inevitably affect educational judgements. When the schooling system itself privileges certain pupils over others, it is hardly surprising that this is reflected in teachers' estimations of ability and attainment. However, the abandonment of such judgements in favour of supposedly objective testing is no solution. The biases built into such assessments are all the more pernicious for their very invisibility. There is, it seems, no way of evading the responsibility of human judgement; and in this, the depth of personal knowledge and reflection on the part of certain teachers, so far from contaminating things, carries the greatest potential for justice. It is the capacity for seeing children in the round – rather than, for instance, in terms that stereotype them by their social class – that enables escape from familiar kinds of bias. For just as the highest forms of thinking may be those that take the fullest account of human particulars, so teachers who recognise the unique identities of the pupils they teach are likely to make the truest assessments of their educational strengths and weaknesses.

Official sorting and grading for competence, as this is officially defined, is a process that is applied not only to pupils, but also to their schools. OFSTED, the Office for Standards in Education, is charged with responsibility for assessing how effectively every educational institution is maintaining 'proper' standards. For schools, their teachers and their pupils, a visit from the OFSTED inspection team carries fateful consequences. Being labelled a 'failing school' can mean an externally appointed new head teacher, together with the sacking of existing members of staff. In line with a policy of 'naming and shaming', the identities of such schools are deliberately publicised in the mass media.

As many children could attest, public humiliation is a strategy apt to backfire. The use of ridicule in class – showing up a pupil in front of friends and classmates – does not produce compliance. Such policies arouse only bitterness and resentment. If this is true of young people in the classroom, it is equally the case where institutions are concerned. The attempt to undermine, to demolish any pride in institutional identity, is likely to be met with anger; and this is generally all the stronger because such judgements are felt to be arbitrary.

OFSTED visits, however brief, often create institutional havoc: preparations and arrangements interrupt the timetable and the curriculum. More fundamentally, the inspection itself is typically felt to stand at odds with the school's own purposes. Judgements are made on bases that have not been negotiated with the staff whose lessons are at issue. Since their criteria are standardised they make no accommodation with the particularities of individual schools. Yet, as has been suggested in the discussion of schools as institutions, it is such particular features as intake, neighbourhood, resources and school culture that guide and constrain any school's educational purposes. To the extent that official judgements from on high ride roughshod over such crucial individual characteristics, even schools rated 'effective' may feel that their own aims, their own real achievements, have been overlooked.

6

School Knowledge

'Shattered and flung about like the splinters of a broken jam-jar, how can all this superficial knowledge be gathered into the swelling, fluctuating flow of life which must have been there?' (Blishen, 1969). This verdict on her history lessons, offered to Edward Blishen by a fourteen-year-old girl, probably expresses many young people's feelings about their school curriculum. The knowledge presented in classrooms seems all too often dead: inert bits of disconnected information, having no relation to the vital business of living.

Children are natural-born learners: think of the teenage fan who knows every phrase, every nuance, of her pop group's latest hit; the ten-year-old boy effortlessly picking up the intricacies of a new computer game; the newly arrived Somali girl already able to interpret for her parents. In seeking to understand, to master, what interests and excites them, young people typically show resources of commitment and enthusiasm seldom seen in older people. But such efforts are applied to spheres and functions that seem to offer some way of enlarging vital concerns, and which therefore exercise real personal pull: the latest achievement of one's *own* pop group, for example, and its reflected glory; the opportunity for demonstrating one's skill, and extending it, in a much-respected technological sphere; the possibility of communicative entry into a whole social world, in which one's peers are already full participants. These kinds of knowledge appeal directly; they have an immediate connection with personal identity, personal agency. And it is this sense of connection that makes for understanding, for intellectual ownership, for meaningfulness.

The secondary school pupils who talk about their classroom learning with Jean Rudduck and her colleagues (1996) repeatedly refer to a sense of incomprehension, to feelings of being lost. For many, this has come to be something they anticipate in school; they do not expect to understand the work. Sometimes this is a matter of not having grasped particular concepts crucial to the particular subject: the idea of circuits in science, for instance, or of grids in geography. These basic holes in understanding are not confined to the 'less able'. As a member of a top set remarks, new material is often explained once only – 'If you don't get it the first time you get left behind'. And being defined as academically able makes it 'hard to admit you haven't got it'.

Being able to learn depends on a sense of the connectedness of learning material, but for these 'learners', discontinuity is a recurring theme. When project work finishes the material is presented in abstract terms and pupils can find no connection between the two. A new teacher takes a distinctive line – in her lessons, the previous subject is unrecognisable. Or, transferred to a new set, a particular pupil encounters disparate content, different tasks.

If within the context of a single subject the knowledge being presented lacks unity, things are often much worse when it comes to coherence across the curriculum. Whereas the primary school timetable allows for the development of at least some cross-curricular themes, for secondary students a sense of fragmentation is typical. School learning, so young people tell Jean Rudduck and her colleagues, consists of a day-long series of short unrelated sessions. There is no sense of lessons fitting together, of any overall coherence in the material presented in their various classrooms.

If school knowledge is generally felt to be arbitrary and disconnected, this is sometimes mitigated by active modes of learning. Field trips and school outings, so say these young people, help them cross boundaries – make connections between school subjects, and between classroom learning and personal experience. A project on local pollution brings science and economics into relation with one's own known neighbourhood. In oral history the previously dead study of the past is suddenly transformed into real people and their actual lives.

Currently, active modes of learning constitute the exception rather than the rule. The heavy demands of the National Curriculum leave little space for this kind of work, while politically inspired pressures endorse a return to traditional teaching modes. Yet where young people are enabled to take at least some control of their own learning, to work from their own resources, to function as active agents rather than merely passive sponges, the outcomes are often highly positive.

Active learning opportunities offer pupils responsibility and convey respect; they treat children as already knowledge-able and resourceful members of society. And they invite young people to engage with curricular material through their own interests, their own purposes. Writing, for instance, that familiar classroom task, typically takes the form of a generalised abstract assignment. But as Douglas Barnes (1986) showed, it becomes a far more fertile exercise if it forms part of a meaningful personal project. Writing to an MP or a newspaper about a real local issue, pupils work with energy and creativeness. Constructing a booklet about 'Our School', for actual use with first formers, or to inform refugee children: this makes far more demands on the imaginative and expressive resources of young writers, and has far greater appeal to real concerns, than the typical decontextualised classroom essay. Here is Stephen, talking retrospectively about his writing with Peter Woods (Woods, 1996). 'You had to be given a task and you had to do it, and the teacher would look at the spelling, that sort of thing . . . It taught me that's not what writing was about at all . . . There's no point in writing something down if you're not going to mean what you say . . . You've got to feel inside that you're telling the truth' (Woods, 1996, p. 130).

In much of the adult Western world, traditional forms of writing have been replaced by electronic communication. This is a mode in which, like that of television and video, most young people feel entirely at home. It is through these modes, with their fast-moving imagery, their acccess to changing information bases and culturally diverse worlds, that the young characteristically learn, really learn, about life. By comparison, the chalk and blackboard of school classrooms, their badly duplicated worksheets, their old, often battered texts, must seem unbelievably outdated. Since young people are particularly sensitive to style, these aspects probably increase still further the irrelevance of school learning.

Widespread and severe resource deprivation obliges teachers to use old-fashioned modes that may invite disrespect from pupils. Still more fundamentally, traditional, instructional styles of teaching forestall the active engagement of learners, without which lessons will not 'take'. But active modes of learning have had a bad press. They have come to be identified with 'progressive' methods: the supposed resort of woolly-minded, idealistic teachers. Mocking reference is made to the 1960s, to the idea that, left to their own devices, children would pick up all they needed to know through so-called discovery learning.

However, participatory forms of learning do not, of course, depend up on the naïve assumption that, given the appropriate resources, learners can do it all by themselves. As the Russian psychologist Lev Vygotsky (1987) argues, education entails access to one's own culture. In this, the involvement of other people is fundamental. Any new competence is acquired through the mediation of some more knowledgeable person; needing help to start with, gradually we become able to manage things for ourselves.

Active learning involves the engagement of minds. Knowledge of the world does not come about through simple hands-on contact. Rather, it is a question of access to what the American educationist Jerome Bruner (1996) has called the system of canonical beliefs. Children, as he argues, learn by thinking: by testing their ideas against the stored knowledge of the culture at large. If they are to develop intellectually, the way young people see things must be taken into account, treated with respect. But that does not mean that anything goes. Purely personal thinking, idiosyncratic and arbitrary interpretations: these cannot stand against what, on the best available evidence so far, is taken to be known.

From this point of view, learning is a matter of bringing the learner's ideas into relation with the shared frame of reference that constitutes current cultural knowledge. Of necessity, this means active participation on the part of those involved. Only by expressing their own viewpoints, articulating their own understandings, can pupils discover where they stand in relation to generally agreed knowledge. Nor can they begin to try out new ways of seeing things simply by being told to do so. For this requires thinking, and thinking, as Michael Billig insists, demands not the imposition of authority, but argument and debate.

If we see school knowledge as enabling access to the wider culture, then the various subjects of the curriculum take on meaning as representing particular ways of seeing and doing things that are shared within the community. Here is Bruner:

> Ways of thinking in mathematics, history, geography or whatever, have developed to achieve certain ways of understanding the world. Unless the child *practises* the role of being a mathematician, historian or geographer, learns the issues that excite such people, the problems that interest them, and the tools that help them to resolve and solve these, then the child may only learn empty tricks and procedures and will not inherit the *discipline* itself (Bruner, 1996, p. 84).

Where they can within the schooling system, many teachers do in fact encourage pupils to take the role of active practitioners. In history, for example, young people work on the available documentary evidence. Taking into account, as far as they can, the situations and perspectives of those who lived at the time, they arrive at their own interpretations and evaluations of recorded events. The understanding acquired through adopting this active stance is quite unlike what may come merely through being told about historical events.

This approach to learning invites learners to feel confident rather than intimidated. It tells them the curriculum is theirs, not just the property of experts. In this, it bypasses the alienation entailed in material sensed to belong – through its language, its style, its social connotations – to groups that are 'other'. But if modes such as these are typically fertile for the learner, they carry all kinds of dangers for conventional practices of education.

Traditionally, the content of school learning is predetermined. The National Curriculum lays down broad guidelines. Within these, it is for teachers to specify where limits shall be drawn: what areas lie within and outside the scope of classroom work. But when pupils take the role of academic practitioner, there can be no such limitation. 'Being' a scientist means applying scientific ideas to the concerns of one's own personal world. No longer an abstruse language, a set of abstract formulations relating to unknowable spheres, science can become a way of thinking about real-life problems. Young people may then demand that it addresses questions uncomfortable for establishment assumptions and practices. Technology-driven priorities in medical research, the role of agri-business in the spread of BSE, government policies towards the environment: such issues, with their human implications, can insist on their right to be heard, can refuse to be excluded from classroom debate.

If the concerns of young people themselves are likely to break down the traditional, safe, limits of school science, this is still more to be expected where the curriculum entails social spheres. For a pupil who takes the study of geography seriously, the world-wide distribution of resources may not make sense without considering Third World exploitation. Economics, on its side, may have to encompass such topics as the power of the military–industrial complex, or the practices of financial speculation and the sale of junk bonds. Nor can history, perhaps, evade its own difficult issues: colonialism, for instance, or the 'interests' governing British foreign policy. These issues may also not stop there, but ramify into questions about the present-day social order. That order, of course, is the explicit focus of social studies;

and here, young people are likely to call into question all sorts of practices, ranging from the treatment of homelessness to a tax system that privileges the 'haves' over the 'have-nots'.

Where scientific knowledge has high social consensus, 'knowledge' about human affairs is far more pluralistic. Social realities are multiple, and contested. There is no single system of canonical truths. We may generally agree about the laws of gravity; but as to human rights or the causes of social breakdown, there are fundamental divergences. Any version of social reality necessarily derives from a particular human standpoint. It carries the perspective, the purposes, the assumptions, the values, associated with that standpoint. Orthodox truths are those of dominant groups, but the many subcultures that constitute our fragmented society have their own, very different, social realities.

To encourage young people to bring real-life concerns into the discussion of their school subjects is to invite challenges, at every point, to the official versions of truth enshrined in the curriculum. Breaking through the smooth, bland surface of the standard textbooks, pupils may insist on their own different situations and experiences, their own, distinctive agendas. Questioned from the standpoint of actual lives, the narrow limitations of the school curriculum cannot but be exposed.

Perhaps nowhere are these limitations more evident than in literary and linguistic spheres of the curriculum. This is true even in the earliest years of schooling, where many reading books still portray human life in highly stereotyped ways. The two-parent family form depicted, where father goes to the office and mother stays at home, is probably unfamiliar to most young children in any classroom. The absence of other than white skins, the traditionally distinctive activities and futures of boys and girls, implicitly marginalise and devalue large numbers of pupils. To working-class children, the essentially middle-class lifestyle often presented must seem personally remote.

These kinds of bias have, over the last decade or so, been the target of concern for certain groups of teachers, particularly those committed to anti-racist and anti-sexist action. But to the extent that much classroom teaching still relies on books portraying a single and atypical version of human possibility, they cannot but alienate the young readers who find no reference to their own identities and experience.

The privileging of white middle-class realities, to the exclusion of others, is not just confined to early forms of school literacy. Texts selected for the English curriculum and the examination syllabus are characteristically white Anglocentric, disregarding the many subcultures of contemporary British society and passing over the rich resources of literature from other cultures.

If this feature typifies literacy in the school curriculum, it is equally, and perhaps more disastrously, the case in the sphere of language. Within any school classroom, and especially in inner-city areas, there is likely to be a huge variety in the language that children use. Not merely are there variations, by class, ethnicity and region, in spoken English itself; many pupils have a non-English first language. According to at least one early official pronouncement, this linguistic diversity was something to be welcomed:

Linguistic diversity is an asset. It provides an opportunity for pupils to gain first-hand experience, knowledge and understanding of other cultures and perspectives. It also helps to prepare pupils for life in a multicultural society by promoting respect for all forms of language. Variety of language is a rich resource which schools should use as they implement the National Curriculum (National Curriculum Council, 1991).

Only two years after the issuing of this document, institutional policy had made a complete U-turn. As the *Guardian* newspaper reported in April 1993, the chairman of the National Curriculum Council 'not only expects teachers to correct children who fail to use Standard English in any lesson or in the playground, but also that they should use Standard English when talking to each other' (*Guardian*, 10 April 1993). The insistence upon one form of language is not just to apply in the classroom; even the most personal and informal talk between young people themselves is to be strictly policed.

Apologists for this kind of approach to pupil language argue that Standard English is exactly that: standard. But standard is a 'weasel' word, suggest Jill Bourne and Deborah Cameron in a discussion of English as a school subject (Bourne and Cameron, 1996). Typically, the justification for official policy slips between two meanings. On the one hand, standard denotes something ordinary and common to all. But the version of language being prescribed is clearly not the way everyone speaks. On the contrary, it is identified with a particular, privileged social class, and as such belongs to a minority of speakers.

Faced with the essentially arbitrary nature of this linguistic prescriptiveness, advocates of Standard English tend to appeal to the other meaning of standard. This defines a particular form of language as inherently desirable, 'the best that has been said and written in our language'. But this is equally arbitrary. As William Labov demonstrated two decades ago, the linguistic medium of Black American English is no less rich, fluent or complex than supposedly better forms, equally structured by its own grammatical rules, and no less effective in its communicative power. It is clearly only from the standpoint of a particular group of speakers that Standard English appears superior. In some circles ideas such as these have come under attack. Many teachers would themselves challenge the notion of a single 'correct' form of language. In some schools in the USA, indeed, 'black' English is actually taught in the classroom. But in our own currently dominant educational ideology – an ideology anchored in the National Curriculum – Standard English remains entrenched.

In the context of schooling, we tend to think of language as a subject, an area of the curriculum for children to study; but of course language is far more than this. It is through talk that we enter the whole human world, that we establish our most significant, our most intimate, personal relationships. Our very identity is vested in the language we use, as witness the blood shed over the linguistic rights of oppressed peoples and the strenuous attempts at linguistic suppression by colonising powers.

Official policies towards school English may sound benign. The insistence upon 'standard' forms appears to represent a means of access to communicative competence, to opportunities in education and employment. But the reality, for the great mass of non-standard speakers, is likely to be disabling: a silencing of spontaneity and a sense of personal and cultural insult, an implicit demeaning not just of pupils themselves, but of their families, homes and backgrounds.

Discussed in narrowly academic terms, language seems merely one more aspect of school knowledge that pupils should acquire. But the essentially social and cultural criteria involved in its evaluation are nowhere more apparent than in relation to minority languages; for whereas a pupil's knowledge of Latin is seen to signify educational competence, fluency in Punjabi is regarded as essentially problematic, a handicap in school learning. This differential judgement reflects not the intellectual status of the language, but the social status, the cultural prestige, of its speakers.

Over the last two decades or so, the determined efforts of an alliance of teachers and academics have forced a general recognition of the plight of children whose first language is not English. Teaching, in the early years, through the medium of the child's home language, is now – at least in principle – general practice. But this does not carry any particular respect for the cultural traditions and resources associated with that language. An absolutist approach to knowledge precludes viewing a Bangladeshi or a Somali young person as the possesser of another, potentially enriching, way of knowing the world. On the contrary, the pupils concerned are seen as culturally deficient; and because language is considered without reference to its social and historical root-edness, the position of such children in relation to the curriculum itself is disregarded. Yet for a child growing up in a practising Muslim household, much of the material presented in the classroom is likely to be irrelevant, if not downright unacceptable. Taken-for-granted assumptions about acceptable foods and their production, about clothes and ways of covering the body, may cut across fundamental values. This basic cultural gulf is, however, typically viewed not in terms of an ethnocentric curriculum, but as showing a deficiency in the child.

English is the medium of classroom instruction. If they are to progress in schooling – to manage their school lives and acquire certification of educational competence – young people from linguistic minorities must learn to speak and write it. But it is hardly surprising if, as they struggle to master a curriculum presented in a foreign medium, their achievement falls at first below that of their native classmates. However, taken together with inescapable problems in communicating with teachers, this inevitable lag is generally seen as denoting innate learning disabilities. All too often this results in relegation to the sphere of 'special educational needs': such pupils are over-represented in sectors associated with low academic achievement.

As Erica Burman (1994) points out, this situation is paradoxical. Bilingual children – children who can speak in more than one language – are typically seen as educationally problematic. The greater flexibility of thought enabled by this learning, the freedom from attachment to a single worldview: these undoubted intellectual assets are completely passed over in the parochial and inward-looking educational perspective currently dominant. Yet in fact, as another writer has scathingly suggested, it is surely monolingualism itself that constitutes the problem: 'Monolingualism is a psychological island. It is an ideological cramp. It is an illness, a disease which should be eradicated' (Skutnabb Kangas, 1988, p. 13). To take this view would recast linguistic minority pupils as the possessors of intellectual resources, of thinking skills unavailable to the majority of English-speaking children – or of English speaking adults, come to that.

For all too many pupils, the classroom curriculum must seem to ignore what they themselves know, to pass it over as essentially worthless. Their language, their situation, their experience may find no place in what is taught. The knowledge offered does not recognise them as already conversant and responsible members of the social world, casting them instead as absolute beginners. Paradoxically, this situation gets worse as schooling progresses. At primary level, a relatively open curriculum allows at least some negotiation with the experience of young learners; but secondary classroom learning, tightly constrained as it is by the examination syllabus, leaves little room for this kind of accommodation. This can mean, for young men and women in their final school years, an experience of classroom work as having not the slightest connection with the vital business of their out-of-school lives.

Yet even within the tight constraints and heavy pressures of the current system, places can still sometimes be found for a very different kind of teaching: one that respects its pupils as knowledgeable and experienced, and builds on their interests, their commitments, their personal and social resources. One such sphere is media studies. Here, the material of learning is not the remote, uninteresting stuff of most school texts, but the images, songs or commercial messages of popular culture. In this sphere, young people are already authorities, with well-developed critical powers and a sophisticated understanding of modes. As such, they can be expected to take an active, expert part: decoding language, identfying ideology – in other words reading between the lines.

Applied cultural studies, one branch of this area, goes further. Phil Cohen (1989), who has pioneered this form of learning, describes its use with a group of working-class pupils in their last year at school in Hackney. Not merely exploring, analysing the representations of others, these young people are encouraged to create their own images of social contexts critical to their lives. Through the use of cameras and tape recorders, they document a number of home and work sites, and build up a portrait of personally significant people, places and activities. The importance of this enterprise as 'preparation for adult life' will be discussed in the final chapter, but in terms of the relevance of school work to real personal concerns, this project has no less significance.

The work entailed in this venture into cultural studies is, as Cohen describes, essentially collective. Though the images assembled by members of the group are individually created, their meaning is communally debated, as are questions about their order in any sequence, or the choice of captions to be added, in the public exhibition representing the project's final outcome. The young people had not formed a social group prior to this learning project, but through their engagement they become so. With an enthusiasm totally absent from their usual classroom activities, they gradually take on responsibility for the work, dismissing their tutors' chaperoning. For each young person there develops a sense of personal involvement, a personal stake in this collective endeavour.

This kind of learning approaches personal and social issues, not in the top-down way typical of most classrooms, but bottom-up. The young people involved do not debate issues abstractly, in purely intellectual terms. Instead, they enter into the social contexts, the engagements and predicaments of their actual or potential lives, and represent their meaning for them. The questions they ask of these contexts are unlikely to be the official ones of social and political education; but in putting these questions, they begin to articulate, question and develop their own common-sense understandings. This is work with the real stuff of living.

In this particular project, Cohen chose a 'silent majority' of pupils: those who, being neither particularly bright nor particularly troublesome, tend to be ignored by busy teachers. Their cultural studies work enables them, as he describes, to bring into play not just a capacity to think, but resources of humour and imagination that remain unelicited in years and years of classroom work. This can mean finding their own voice for the first time: 'Not by shouting loudest, but by listening and putting into words what has been silenced by what they have been made to echo' (Cohen, 1997a, p. 403).

Alas, this situation is far from typical of school-based learning. The institutional pressures that weigh on teachers no less heavily than on their pupils make for immense difficulties in carrying through the kind of project undertaken by Cohen. Yet where, rarely, conditions allow it, education becomes transformed. Given opportunities and resources for exploring their own vital questions, even potentially disaffected young people can commit themselves, take responsibility, and learn – *really* learn – for themselves.

7

Classroom Converse

The following passage is from an interview conducted with an adolescent male pupil by Gillian Brown and her colleagues (Brown *et al.*, 1984). Like others in this study, the boy was judged by his teachers to be within the lower third of his year in academic ability. The pupil is telling the interviewer about the difference between the film *Jaws* and the book it is based on:

> *Interviewer*: 'Is the book like the film?'
> *Pupil*: '. . . A wee bit.'
> *Interviewer*: 'Hmmm . . . What's different in the book?'
> *Pupil*: 'In the book . . . Hooper dies in the film but he never dies but he went in a cage down . . . to see if he could see the fish . . . and like . . . and trying to get in . . . the fish . . . but he couldn't . . . the fish turned er the cage over but then he went away and Hooper just went and swum out and hid behind a rock and . . . in the book he said that he died.'

In terms of the information it offers, this account is obviously deficient. As a narrative it is not coherent; the listener ends up none the wiser about the difference between the book and the film. This does not mean that the speaker is incapable of talking effectively. Like other members of his 'unacademic' group, when observed chatting with friends he is typically voluble and witty, evidently suffering no communicative problems. But these two speech contexts are, of course, as William Labov insisted three decades ago, significantly different. And in the formality, the artificiality, the judgemental atmosphere of a test interview, the boy fails to produce an adequate account.

Adult–pupil interviews have echoes of school lessons. The peculiarities of classroom converse have already been discussed in relation to the work of Mary Willes. It was Willes (1983) who first drew attention to the differential speaking rights of pupils and teachers, the overwhelming predominance of teacher talk, and the reduction of pupil contributions to purely reactive responses. More recently, other researchers have elaborated these findings. The educationist David Wood (1988), for instance, describes the typical form of talk between teachers and pupils as that of question-answer-acknowledgement.

One of Wood's particular concerns has been the development of oracy: the ability to use spoken language effectively. The influential *Bullock Report* (1977) on language in schools, as he remarks, argued for the importance of this sphere as a legitimate educational goal. Yet in learning to give a verbal account of oneself and what one knows, typical classroom converse could hardly be less facilitative. In part, this is because of the oddity, in human terms, of teachers' questions.

As Wood suggests, questions in everyday life perform a variety of functions. Usually, we ask questions of other

94

people in order to find out something we do not know, but need to know. Teachers, however, typically already have the answers to the questions they put; and pupils, for their part, realise this. More fundamentally, classroom questions violate implicit rules of ordinary social discourse, for conversations have a moral character.

Imagine, asks Wood, a demand from a visitor on your doorstep to know how much you earn. Such an interrogation would be seen as illegitimate; not everyone has the right to ask any question. Requests for information are never entirely neutral. Deciding how far to go in probing for answers is normally a delicate matter; it entails judgements about what is permissible and polite, and what might cause offence. In ordinary life all this is possible because questions are asked in the context of a social relationship in which each person has some sense of the other's social and cultural identity and values.

Learning to be a pupil, as Willes defines it, means understanding and working within the humanly peculiar practices of classroom talk – and of course some pupils manage to do this very well. For those who succeed, there is typically a smaller distance between parents and teachers, between the modes and language of home and school. Their talk in classrooms is not altogether different from their 'natural' way of talking, at home and with their friends – though it is likely to be far more limited, far less rich. The out-of-school converse of other pupils, however, is quite unlike the way they speak in class. Socially and culturally, the two contexts are miles apart for such young people. In responding to teachers, these fluent, witty, articulate talkers become monosyllabic and stilted. And this linguistic 'incompetence' is a fateful one, for classroom oracy is fundamental in judgements about academic ability.

Nor is it only teacherly questions that may act to alienate

pupils. For many young people sitting in the classroom, the language that teachers use itself constitutes an insuperable barrier. In talking and in thinking, we can draw only on familiar terms: terms that make sense to us, terms that are part of our personal currency. But the school curriculum is characteristically framed in its own specialised languages. There are particular ways of speaking about maths, history, science or economics. The ideas, the practices, that these subjects entail are presented in words that have little meaning for many of their recipients. It is only when, through their own empathy and imagination, teachers are able to frame their material in pupils' own linguistic currency, that the subject may begin to make sense.

What this can entail is illustrated in the work of Douglas Barnes (1986), an influential writer about language in the curriculum. Barnes insists that school learning can occur only if it links in with the 'action knowledge' of day-to-day experience. He exemplifies this from a recorded lesson in physics. The class group had been defined as being of low academic ability. Rather than insisting that they master a technical vocabulary, the teacher encourages his pupils to try out their own formulations of what is happening in the experiment. To enable them to do this, he himself speaks in highly untechnical language:

This is almost the same as that one . . . a slightly different arrangement . . . cut in half . . . you see it? . . . little tin can . . . silver thing in the middle . . . silver thing with circles on it? . . . that's that tin can . . . tin can just like that one . . . all right . . . on a good day then what is going to happen to the shape of that? Is it going to go . . . down? . . . Do you know? . . . See what happens to the pointer. Well that pointer is going to be connected . . .

As Barnes describes, the 'unacademic' pupils in this lesson become actively involved in it. They attend closely to the demonstration and question their teacher about what they see. This is surely related to the way he talks. Informal though his language is, it is informative because it is precisely adjusted to the apparatus; but more significantly, the way the teacher talks carries its own message: that he is interested in his pupils' own understandings and their attempts to extend them. In respecting their natural ways of talking, he enables them to engage personally with physics – that typically obscure, remote and alienating subject.

The pupils in Barnes' example are active; they do not merely sit passively, but ask their own spontaneous questions. If learning is to happen, learners have to do something for themselves. They need to participate, to take their own initiatives; and this, as Billig insists, necessarily involves argument and challenge. We move forward in our understanding only through debating unlikely possibilities: trying out contrary positions, confronting established assumptions. In school classrooms such talk is rare indeed. The conventional form of converse – the question-answer-acknowledgement mode – could hardly be more discouraging to it. Classroom talk presupposes linguistic obedience, a compliance with given terms and given positions. Arguing with the teacher, so far from being expected, is typically treated as illegitimate and provocative.

Children's talk in classrooms – so vital for the academic progress they will make, or fail to make – is regarded as an individual accomplishment. Being able to express oneself clearly is, we assume, a personal attribute that some 'able' pupils possess, while others do not. Yet talking is nothing if not a joint endeavour. We talk, not alone, but to and with others. How we say things, and what we say is governed not just by the nature of the person we address, but in a moment-to-moment way by that person's own verbal or tacit responses. Our converse is essentially interactive. Mutual understanding is the responsibility of both participants. And, of course, in the informal contexts of established social relationships, we take constant conversational short-cuts. So much is already understood between us that matters need not be spelt out.

It is surely this relational basis that enables spontaneity in talk. Mutual sympathy with one's audience allows the taking of risks: the expression of feelings, of half-thought-out ideas that may later be reconsidered. With a friend, a known and trusted person, it is possible to try out perhaps absurd positions without losing face, or issue challenges without seeming to be hostile. And it is just these untidy, wayward, sometimes incoherent, ways of talking – quite unlike the formal, polished speech required in classrooms – that allows real thinking to develop.

The sense of social relationship that fosters creative kinds of talk is very difficult to establish in classrooms. Institutions, as suggested previously, characteristically reduce their inmates to anonymity. Being a pupil can all too often mean being lost in the mass. There is typically little sense of personal recognition and respect: 'If Jamie's name is called by the teacher,' writes Phil Cohen 'it is normally only to summon him back to a legal place of attendance as a "pupil", in which nothing that makes him Jamie counts for much' (Cohen, 1997a, p. 374). In the context of answering teachers' questions, young people probably seldom speak from a sense of known and respected personal identity. The teacher to whom they speak is likely to seem equally anonymous: merely a role, a school position.

In talk that is unconstrained, there is a mutuality between speakers, a recognition of joint endeavour, a sense of 'us'. In classrooms, however, talk between pupils and teacher is seldom like this. Rather, it is a matter, on either side, of 'us' versus 'them'. The built-in relations of dominance and subordination that define so much of schooling act to maintain a seemingly impossible distance between the two sets of participants. Yet the gulf can sometimes be bridged. In this, how pupils, as learners, are addressed is crucial.

Our conventional view of learning is one of transmission. We think of it as additive, as involving an incremental growth of more and more knowledge. Teachers, being knowledgeable, instruct; pupils, being ignorant, receive the information purveyed. Teachers are experts, children are ignorant. In this perspective, an us/them distinction is fundamental; and much of schooling is built on this premise. The roles of adults and young people are highly differentiated. The distinction between them is explicitly marked out, not merely in their classroom roles, but in separate spaces, separate facilities, differential forms of dress. All this seems at first sight to be perfectly natural. Children are not, after all, the same as adults; it is only reasonable that schooling should make this difference clear.

The family setting is also one that adults share with children. In that context too, as any parent would attest, children learn and adults teach. Yet the learning relationship, and the modes of teaching, are altogether different from those of school. This difference is not just a matter of the far more intimate personal relations that obtain at home. Beyond this, learning at home entails the sense of shared concerns, of joint endeavour. In teaching their children, parents address them as if they were essentially like themselves; as sharing the same kind of subjectivity. This means seeing even the youngest children in terms of potentiality, rather than limitation.

In their interaction with small babies, mothers talk as though their infants were already quite advanced. They credit them, as it were, with powers of understanding that such young creatures could not possibly possess. This has been established in a number of studies that have recorded, on video, the 'conversations' between mother and baby pairs. These show the adult caretaker, on her part, responding to the movement or the vocalising of an infant as entailing capacities for agency and communication comparable with her own. 'You want to give me the teddy? Oh, thank you!' she says in response to her baby's waving arm. 'Yes, that's a pretty flower, isn't it!' is her comment as she looks in the direction of the infant's gaze. She treats babble as meaningful, though unfinished, language, completing utterances on the baby's behalf.

This kind of communicative response invites even the youngest babies into the subjective world of adults. The invitation is conveyed through the implication that they already inhabit this world: that their rudimentary, perhaps even random movements and sounds represent humanly meaningful gestures and language. And it is precisely through these kinds of 'conversations' that babies do come to acquire the powers with which they have been, in some sense, prematurely credited. For in being treated as more advanced than they actually are, they assimilate meaning; they develop inter-subjectivity.

In their day-to-day relations with their small babies, parents, it seems, naturally treat them as far more capable than that actually are; and it is through these kinds of relations that infants do develop their characteristically human capabilities. Such learning is of a very fundamental kind. It underpins the possibility of all further learning. Yet its modes – the means through which it seems to take place – stand a world away from those that school sets up to foster its own kind of learning.

In the context of mother–baby interaction, communication

rests on a sense of possibility. Primitive responses are seen as containing far greater potential than a literal interpretation would suggest. But in school contexts, the management of learning is based on notions of human limits, of built-in incompetence. The whole system of assessment and certification entails a hierarchy, which places pupils at fixed points beyond which they cannot, supposedly, move. By definition, such ranking further marks out half the school population as failures: as standing below the norm of capability. But still more fundamentally, the conception of what school learning actually means, and the classroom practices that implement this conception, place pupils as incompetent, defining their position in terms of what they cannot do. Unlike the treatment of babies as more capable than they really are, school learning typically treats learners as less able than they feel themselves to be.

When we observe the child's development and instruction in school, it becomes apparent that each subject demands more than the child is capable of, leading the child to carry out activities that force him to rise above himself. This is always the case with healthy school instruction. The child begins to learn to write when he does not yet have the mental functions that are required for written speech. It is for precisely this reason that instruction in written speech calls these functions to life and leads their development (Vygotsky, 1987, p. 213.)

This passage was written in the 1920s by Lev Vygotsky, a Russian psychologist whose ideas have recently been taken up by a number of educational writers. As his words suggest, Vygotsky saw the function of school learning as calling on children's potential, rather than their actual level of accomplishment. Demands should lead learners to 'perform beyond themselves'. They should be invited to participate in activities that they could not yet fully understand: 'it is only by playing the game that they eventually learn the rules'. In this way, as Vygotsky puts it, children come to perform beyond themselves, they act 'ahead of themselves', 'a head taller than they are'.

Vygotsky's vision of school learning is, it seems, inspired by exactly the same principles that intuitively guide parents in their interactions with very young children. Just as mothers attribute to their infants capacities that they do not as yet possess, so teachers, in Vygotsky's portrayal, need to treat their pupils as more competent than they presently are. And just as babies come to acquire the powers of understanding their mothers already see in them, so school learners will grow into the competences with which their teachers credit them.

Such a view could hardly stand in greater contrast with the philosophy which has traditionally governed schooling. That philosophy rests on notions of limitedness. Individual pupils are seen as inhabiting defined points on a continuum of competence: points above which they cannot go. As a constituency, they are defined by ignorance, by a status of not knowing, as against the status of teachers as knowing. Classroom converse, in its constant assumption of teacherly authority, carries a reducing rather than enlarging portrayal of pupil capacity. Quite unlike the generous attributions of parents, schooling typically underestimates its learners. As with any self-fulfilling prophecy, the end result is all too predictable. For just as infants grow into the competent beings their parents see in them, so, in school classrooms, all too many pupils come to live out diminished identities as people of limited capacity.

Yet, as Hartley (1986) shows, even in school test situations young people can respond 'above themselves'. In inviting 'low-ability' pupils to pretend to be clever, Hartley elicits competences these children are supposed not to possess. Where teachers make performance, of any kind, a feature of classroom work, pupils typically rise to the occasion, easily transcending the limited role to which they are traditionally reduced. In dramatic work, for instance, young people often reveal previously hidden gifts of insight. Out of role, it seems, we can all be more than we 'are'.

Not all teachers view their pupils in the traditional and constraining terms of ignorance and incompetence. Despite the institutional apparatus that allocates to learners a reducing rather than an enlarging role, many teachers do address the potential of young people. Their way of talking emphasises not present limitations, but assured soon-to-be acquired abilities. They relate to their pupils in advance of their actual development. In inviting children not merely to receive, but to practise forms of knowledge – to be writers, physicists, geographers, historians, and so on – teachers convey their faith in pupils' possibilities.

This invitation, of itself, transforms classroom converse, for it at once abolishes the gap between learner and teacher. No longer excluded, as ignoramuses from the curriculum sphere at issue, pupils join teachers as practitioners. Talk is no longer top-down, but involves relations of human, if not yet intellectual, equality. 'Us' and 'them' disappear, to become 'we'. Genuine developing kinds of talk become possible – spontaneous, tentative, argumentative. This approach can surely forestall, if anything can, the alienation so many young people feel towards classroom work. For it embodies the respect, the positive recognition – that universal human need – that pupils all too often fail to find in school.

8

Morality and Schooling

Young people are often seen as trouble. Sensationalist reporting by the mass media depicts a lawless generation, uncontainable at school or in the home, high on drugs and given to robbery and street violence. Exceptional cases, such as the murder of Jamie Bulger, are taken as prototype. The prevailing moral panic dictates drastic measures; potential social breakdown can be averted, perhaps, only by street curfews and the electronic tagging of ten-year-old boys.

In this perception, schools, like parents, are seen to carry a heavy responsibility. If children are to grow into decent, responsible citizens, so goes the rhetoric, then the adults charged with their care must teach them the difference between right and wrong. And where the moral 'teaching' of the home takes place in private, at least for most families, that of schools is public, and subject to official prescription and surveillance.

This view has direct and specific implications for schooling. It makes morality into a special kind of knowledge: the knowledge of right and wrong. Its advocates would probably see such knowledge as informing, in a general way, all the subjects of the school curriculum. However, it would be represented more explicitly in the areas covered by Personal and Social Education. Here, through the medium of group discussion, sometimes accompanied by films and videos, teachers are expected to inculcate in young people principles of social responsibility and law-abiding behaviour. In practice, this kind of education has tended to focus on such issues as drink, drugs and smoking. But evidence suggests that its impact, in actually affecting young people's behaviour, is negligible or non-existent. Teachers' exhortations to drink moderately, to refrain from smoking, to reject the drug scene, apparently carry for their pupil audience no real weight.

In this scenario, morality is narrowly viewed: as applying only to certain forms of supposedly proscribed individual behaviour. Human relationships, the way that people treat each other – the contexts to which moral principles might be thought to apply par excellence – these are seen to lie outside the scope of formal schooling. The highly restricted content of sex education is one consequence.

In most current practice, sex education is sometimes a subject in its own right; and sometimes part of the science curriculum. But in both cases, its main content consists of a factual account of the human reproductive process. This does not include information and advice about contraception. Giving such advice to girls under sixteen may even, according to the 1993 Education Act, constitute a criminal offence. Underlying this policy is the rationale that information on contraception would encourage premature sexual activity. This argument does of course ignore the fact that many young people are already sexually active by their early teens. Nor, in its castigation of the risks of teenage pregnancies, can it be squared with an incidence of such events in the UK which is seven times that of the Netherlands, a country with an up-front system of sex education. And, with the now generally acknowledged prevalence of HIV and AIDS, to withhold this kind of information would seem to most people nothing short of irresponsible.

Young people themselves characteristically deplore the lack of helpful information in a vital sphere of their own lives, and view schools as failing in their responsibilities to provide it. But more urgently still, they look to teachers of sex education to enable an exploration of the whole human context of sexual relationships – the social, personal and emotional meanings of sexuality.

We usually think of sexuality as applying only to directly physical relations, yet as a major constituent in the construction of gender, the sexual dimension informs the perceptions of even quite young children. Indeed, such children may sometimes put its connotations to oppressive use. A disconcerting study by Valerie Walkerdine (1981) illustrates this. She records a conversation between three nursery school children, in which the two boys use a sexually abusive term towards both their female classmate and their teacher. Referring to both girl and teacher as 'cunt', 'they bring their teacher down to size; she and a small girl are . . . the same thing – sex objects' (Walkerdine, 1981, p. 16).

The sexual superiority of males is a lesson early learned by girls and boys, and lived out daily in their lives at school. Female pupils (and, not infrequently, their female teachers) are subject to routine verbal and physical harassment. Sexually, they walk a tightrope; both active behaviour and its opposite risk their own kinds of abuse label. This is part of the double standard that identifies male sexuality with prowess, but dubs sexually active girls irresponsible, if not actually depraved. Yet paradoxically, to take sexual responsibility by carrying a condom is itself to invite disapproval.

Nor is it only girls, as girls, who endure the risks endemic in sexual politics. The dominance of heterosexuality, together with pervasive homophobic attitudes, mean the pathologisation of minority sexual orientations. Substantial numbers of gay and lesbian young people in school live each day with the threat or the actuality of persecution: of derision and rejection, of verbal cruelty, of physical violence.

If boys and men are undeniably the more advantaged gender, this does not mean that they suffer no costs. Male identity as itself imprisoning forms part of the subject of a later chapter, as do attempts in school to rework the existing order. That order, however, is unlikely to yield to the kind of education that rests on the explicit teaching of moral principles. For a conception of morality as essentially a matter of thinking and reasoning ignores its character as inseparable from social life.

Advocates of traditional views about human morality often ground their arguments in a particular line of psychological research on moral development. This work, in which the American psychologist Lawrence Kohlberg (1981) played a prominent part, portrays young children as initially amoral, only gradually developing towards moral maturity. In this progression, early forms of morality are essentially conformist, and represent a simple deferring to authority. Later, children begin to evolve their own rules, but conceive them in a somewhat literal and slavish way. Only during late adolescence may young people attain the highest level of morality: abstract, reasoned principles of justice. Rationality, the traditional goal of schooling, is again seen as crucial to the operation of mature moral thinking.

Moral maturity is defined in this portrayal as the adherence to principles of justice, unaffected by the particularities of human context. On this logic, adult social life should, on the whole, be governed by such principles. With increasing age, supposedly, there is a progression towards an impartial ethical stance. Unmoved by any personal considerations, or by their own particular situations in life, mature people make their moral choices purely for the furtherance of equity and social order. But the absurdity of such a supposition is all too evident in our own increasingly unequal society, where a capitalist ethos valorises blatant self-interest, profitability and dog-eat-dog over collective endeavour and the common good.

The depiction of moral development, from amorality to abstract principles of justice, is based on research that asks children to make judgements about a number of moral dilemmas. In one of these, they are presented with a story about a man whose wife will die unless she is given a certain medicine. This medicine is very expensive, and the man has no money to pay for it. Should he steal the medicine? Children's levels of morality are inferred not from the answer yes or no, as such, but from the kind of argument they put forward, the justifications they offer. Their thinking, rather than their conduct, is the focus. In line with the rationalist assumptions underlying this approach, reasoning is thought to underlie action. Young people, in this scenario, make conscious choices before they act, drawing on their repertoire of moral thinking.

Parents sometimes tell their children, 'Do what I say, not what I do.' The gulf between actual conduct and declared beliefs, between private behaviour and publicly professed principles, can surely surprise few people, as witness the barely raised eyebrows at recent revelations of political sleaze. Though we may be adept at later accounting for our actions, how we act in the heat of the moment is likely to be intuitive and unthinking.

Efforts to set up morality as a purely cognitive sphere of education ignore its rootedness in action, in social agency. To recognise this means acknowledging even the youngest children as already members of a moral universe; morality, as Tom Kitwood suggests, 'is not something that is added on later, as a kind of overlay or injection' (Kitwood, 1986, p. 7). In participating in shared decisions on family topics that matter, young children are, in Berry Mayall's term, 'moral interpreters of the world they engage in' (Mayall, 1994, p. 136). If schooling is to engage with moral questions, it can do so only through a recognition of its pupils not as morally ignorant, but as already moral agents.

The traditional view sees moral development as progressing towards a set of abstract, universalised principles. But if morality is not to be divorced from its essentially social rootedness, then it cannot but reflect the differentiated positions and experience of the diverse groups that make up our society. Standards of conduct, proper ways of doing things, right and wrong in human affairs: these are hardly matters of universal consensus – rather, judgement depends on who is talking. Traditions, customs and values vary across cultures and subcultures; there is no single moral code.

Nor do we, as individuals, base our social actions on a rational and explicit moral code. So far from following a coherent and logically consistent set of ethical principles, human conduct is characteristically inconsistent, full of double standards, ambiguities and contradictions. A group of unemployed men, talking with Sara Wilmott and Christine Griffin (1997) formulate a view of 'fiddling' as a course of action quite distinct from stealing.

> The men made a distinction here between 'casual' work or 'fiddling' to survive and augment the dole, and real 'thieving', in a parallel with the distinction between 'idle scroungers' and 'genuine claimants'. Just as they all constructed themselves as 'genuine claimants' rather than 'idle scroungers', those that admitted to 'fiddling' never presented

themselves as 'proper criminals' (Wilmott and Griffin, 1997, pp. 123–4).

As this example shows, how we conduct ourselves is intimately linked with who we are. It is our social situation, our social identity, that governs our behaviour. Through the process of osmosis that brings about lived understandings, young children pick up the assumptions and expectations that apply to 'their' kind of person. Their membership of family and peer groups, their participation and engagements in the business of those groups, implicitly teach them how the world is, how things are done, and what it means to be a girl, a black person, or a middle-class boy.

School is a world of diverse pupil identities. Not only do children bring to their classrooms and playgrounds very different social situations, life experience, expectations and standards of behaviour, but within the arena of school itself new identities come to be forged. Of course official judgements of educational competence serve to differentiate pupils, but ultimately more significant are the relations of domination and subordination among young people themselves, established most visibly through bullying.

Bullying practices, at all levels of schooling, have for some time been the focus of public and institutional concern. The intensity of personal distress on the part of some pupils, sometimes even leading to suicide, has shocked those who had seen schools as safe places for children. Efforts to counter this kind of behaviour are now widespread, with whole-school policies towards bullying now being the rule rather than the exception. A number of consultative bodies have been set up to advise on strategies.

Institutional efforts to deal with bullying now use a wide range of methods. Most schools have a reporting policy; every incident witnessed by staff or pupils must be officially notified and logged. Codes of conduct, which pupils help to draw up, may be established, and violations, together with sanctions, are recorded and discussed. Actual or potential bullying situations are acted out dramatically in role play, with subsequent class debate. Some schools have schemes for peer counselling. Others use mediation: bully and victim confront each other in the presence of two fellow-pupils to bridge communication.

All these strategies have a common denominator. They approach bullying as a product of special interpersonal contexts. In examining a particular incident – of racist name-calling, say – pupils are encouraged to consider the particular behaviour involved, by both parties, and to think of other ways in which each might have responded. The personal tendencies of bullies and victims are discussed, together with the choices available to both. The philosophy guiding these strategies is one that views bullying in essentially individualised terms.

A perspective on pupil–pupil relations as a function of individual characteristics and behaviour ignores the fact that young people, in their classroom and playground encounters, do not meet as equals. Children live their lives in a wider social world where power and privilege are unevenly distributed. If dominance and subordination mark the relationships of young people from the start of schooling to its final years, this is scarcely surprising. Nor is it merely an accident that many of those whose school lives are lived in a climate of fear, loneliness and intimidation tend to belong to social groups that are characteristically disadvantaged. Conversely, white middle-class children may be picked on in schools with a predominantly working-class pupil population.

From this viewpoint, bullying appears not as a product of the inappropriate behaviour of a few particular individuals needing re-education, but as one aspect of the power relations pervading a society of which children are part. Nor can schools themselves, as also part of that wider society, be left out of this account. Reflecting, as to some extent they must, the values and assumptions of socially dominant groups, they are all too likely to be living out the same power relations that govern pupil bullying.

In this rather different philosophy, bullying is not a specific problem belonging to particular pupils, but merely one aspect of the whole social order, which the school itself may be implicitly endorsing. Do institutional structures embody the privileging of certain groups over others, with white middle-class men in positions of authority? How democratic is the running of the school, and does it reflect the views of less powerful staff members? Is staffroom culture permeated by sexist jokes and the 'playful' harassment of women teachers? What sort of discipline system operates, and do pupils see it as fair or arbitrary? How far does the 'labelling' of pupils reflect adverse stereotypes of gender and 'racial' groups?

Looked at like this, name-calling, harassment and violence among chilldren cannot be divorced from the institutional context in which it takes place. For all the virtuous slogans embodied in official policies, pupils may be learning a very different lesson from the power relations actually operating in their school world. The hidden agenda, conveyed in the day-to-day practices of teachers and auxiliary staff, may be offering a message that endorses rather than counters social relations of oppression and victimisation.

It is on the basis of these kinds of assumption that some recent school initiatives have been formulated. Rather than adopting strategies that focus on individual pupils, these approaches pay careful attention to what Stephen Ball (1987) has called the micro-politics of the school. As Ball argues, every school has its own ideology, which profoundly affects the organisation and teaching of pupils, the relationships between teachers and pupils, and the whole pattern of decision-making. Nor, of course, are schools hermetically sealed from the wider world, but increasingly subject to external, often contradictory, pressures. Consequent staff overload can make for difficulty, even in the most sympathetic school climate, when new approaches to classroom teaching come to be introduced.

Debbie Epstein (1993), an anti-racist teacher and researcher, sees all these aspects as crucial to the success of her own work. In the various initiatives she has launched in the primary sector, she works at a number of institutional levels. As potentially vital supporters, the head and the opinion leaders in the school must be enlisted as allies. By the same token, those staff who might act as 'blockers' must be identified.

It is of course teachers themselves who act as the instruments of educational change. And this, necessarily, means work at the level of professional training, through in-service courses. For, like the rest of us, members of the teaching profession may have only limited understandings of 'other' groups.

One misconception portrays the cultures of black people as static and unchanging:

In practice, of course, all of us live within and in relation to a variety of 'cultures', which change and which we ourselves alter through our activities. Moreover, teachers who make assumptions about the 'home culture' of children in their classes on the basis of names, religion, colour or place or origin are almost certain to get it wrong. Children in Birmingham, white or black, are, for example, equally likely to eat 'Indian' food or fish and chips. Religious observance changes over time and from family to family. Language too changes, and English and minority languages are influenced by each other (Epstein, 1993, p. 145).

But it is perhaps at the level of direct teacher–pupil contact that the most crucial work has to be done. If teachers are to rework oppressive relations between pupils, a new kind of classroom order needs to be established. At one level, this means opening up the classroom to the wider world. In her class of five- and six-year-old children, Epstein, in common with a growing number of teachers, routinely involves parents: reading, helping, talking about the stories. For those unable or unwilling to come, she takes care to talk about her anti-racist concerns, either after school or at parents' evenings. This has meant confronting some initial hostility over the focus on 'race' in a class of all-white children, and, in other cases, reassuring anxious parents that such work does not imply an inattention to 'basics'.

Bringing in parents, allowing them active roles, discussing and negotiating educational aims: all this helps to ensure that teachers' efforts are supported, as far as possible, by the much more important culture of the home. But in seeking to open up the classroom confines, to widen the scope of its lessons, many teachers regularly invite other kinds of visitors from the non-school world. Epstein describes how one black writer, Grace Hallworth, tells stories to her first-year class, and talks to the children about books. Do their own reading books have pictures of people like her, she asks. This leads to a search in the class library, in which not merely omissions are considered, but accuracy and 'fairness' in the depiction of black people.

But most fundamentally the development of more equal and less oppressive relations amongst pupils calls for a classroom climate in which young people feel safe to express their feelings. Autocratic teachers may succeed in forestalling the slightest expression of racist or sexist attitudes during lessons, but out in the corridor or playground abuse and violence will continue unabated. Only if pupil–teacher relations have achieved sufficient openness and mutual trust are young people likely to risk revealing feelings that are officially proscribed. Without such expression, the real agenda of social relations will remain outside the scope of education.

It is, however, at this point that teachers need to act in particularly delicate ways. For those committed to the establishment of equality and respect among pupils, oppressive language and behaviour cannot go unchallenged. But teacherly hectoring and heavy-handed moralising can only alienate their recipients. What is called for is a dialogue that draws on the ideas of children themselves. By reminding young people of what they themselves have said, and by amplifying some of its unstated implications, it is sometimes possible to suggest alternative ways of looking at the world.

This sort of possibility, and how it is actually missed by one particular teacher, is exemplified in a conversation recorded by Epstein. A class teacher (C. J.) is talking with a small group of eleven-year-old children, of whom Kuldeep and Gurdial are Sikh, Rachel is white and Scottish, and Anne is white and from the West Midlands:

Gurdial: 'My dad came first and then my mum. But they wasn't married when he came. He came back to India to get married and then they came here together.'
C. J.: 'Did they have any problem with coming?'
Kuldeep: 'Well, my mum, she said it was really horrible. Because she had to wait so long, and then it took ages, when there was enough money, it took ages to get a . . . umm, a, what's it called?'
C. J.: 'A visa?'

Kuldeep: 'I think so [unintelligible] lots of questions – like when she got married and if my dad was really her husband and that . . .'

Anne: 'But that's not fair! She wouldn't say he was her husband if he wasn't.'

C. J.: 'Why do you think the immigration officer asked her those questions?'

Kuldeep: 'Something, something to do with the law.'

C. J.: 'Do you know anything about the law, immigration law?'

Kuldeep: 'Well, my dad says it's something about not wanting so many Indian people here. He says it's because of racism.'

Rachel: 'Yes, but when there's lots of people, English people, without jobs, you can understand . . .'

Anne: 'But you're not English either. You said your mum and dad and you, you came from Scotland.'

C. J.: 'Perhaps we should try to find out more about the immigration laws. I think Mrs Epstein has got some books, or maybe we could get something from the library.'

As Epstein remarks, in this conversation Rachel repeats the familiar formulation that black people come to England to take jobs that rightfully belong to the English. This is half-challenged by Anne, another white girl, who points out that Rachel is not English herself. But instead of developing the implications of this, and perhaps enabling the children to re-think current mythologies about black immigration, the teacher closes down the conversation. Controversy in the classroom, as Epstein suggests, is hard to handle; 'teachers are trained to try to avoid conflict'. Yet morality can only be reworked to the extent that the implicit ground rules of social relations, with all their divisive potential, are voiced by children themselves.

What might be involved in such a reworking is illustrated in a recent project conducted by Phil Cohen (1997b). Unlike that of most research studies in school, its focus is the playground. As Cohen argues, school playgrounds constitute an arena of significant interactions between young people, where the world of the adult community and its institutional regimes carry little weight. And despite the ostensibly 'innocent' character of children's play, much playground activity involves conflict, teasing and harassment. Boys aggressively commandeer territory, leaving girls only marginal space. Many games entail exclusion, often on a racist basis. Under the guise of play, unpopular pupils can be bullied unmercifully. Cruel taunts masquerade as fun: the perpetrator 'a sadistic wind-up merchant who is only ever joking', with the butt cast as someone unable to take a joke.

Cohen's project involves an Infant and Junior school situated in London's Docklands, with pupils from a wide diversity of social and cultural backgrounds. Video recordings are made of playground activity, and excerpts of these shown to groups of children, teachers and playground supervisors, who discuss the events they see. Alongside the variety of differing interpretations that these discussions elicit, one theme that emerges is the sheer complexity of relations, within this arena, between children and adults. In episodes of racist or sexist harassment, for instance, few pupils appeal to teachers or supervisors. Talking about this, children are generally agreed that such reports are unlikely to be believed, and carry the dire risk of being labelled a tell-tale. Playground supervisors, in any case, are seen to carry little authority: a perception endorsed by their status in school as poorly paid women assistants, with minimal career opportunities, whose functions are merely ancillary.

With his colleagues, Cohen sets out to open up the world of the playground, to make it responsive to the active intentions of its child and adult participants. One strategy entails reducing the cultural gulf between classroom and playground, building bridges between the two spheres, particularly through story telling. Other new practices apply directly to playground events.

Basic rules are established, through classroom discussion, as to the 'policing' of behaviour, with an agreed division of responsibility between staff and pupils. These include working out a consensus on what constitutes minor or major incidents, and on what action would be appropriate in each case. The reporting of incidents, previously the sole province of supervisory staff, is to include signed statements by protagonists and eye witnesses; in this way a variety of perspectives are to be involved, rather than a simple value judgement made from one adult position. These reports are to be submitted to the School Council, a pupil forum in which issues about harassment and bullying are seriously debated. As Cohen describes, such discussions prove valuable, with the establishment, for instance, of a time share system ensuring that younger children get their fair share of the play apparatus.

In implementing all these changes, playground supervisory staff are given a crucial role, in contrast with their previous marginalisation in discussions of school policies. For despite the low status generally accorded to these women, by pupils and teaching staff alike, they hold a potentially significant position as adult representatives in often momentous playground encounters.

In current rhetoric, schools have a duty to teach children the difference between right and wrong. This simplistic formulation entirely passes over the complex nature of human morality. This is not just because it depicts children as morally not-yet, as blank sheets waiting to be inscribed with ethical beliefs. It also denies the fundamentally problematic character of morality. For the relation between social action and moral beliefs is far from straightforward. This is not to suggest that we regularly act in bad faith. It is rather that what we do arises out of our particular social positions, our expected, habitual and generally unquestioned relationships with others. Not merely are our actions frequently at variance with our professed morality; they may often also be mutually contradictory.

The single, universally acceptable moral code that schools are supposed to offer cannot in any case be squared with the wide diversity of moralities within our own society. While explicit ethical principles may bear only a loose relation to much of day-to-day behaviour, nevertheless they prescribe certain positions and practices that are highly significant to their believers. As recent history has shown, institutional regimes that ride roughshod over the dress codes or dietary requirements of non-Christian pupils can arouse outraged rebellion. The refusal of many teachers to carry out traditional forms of school assembly arises from a recognition of the validity of alternative religions.

The notion of moral education inevitably poses the question: whose morality is to be promoted? Given that the school constituency encompasses our entire, hugely diverse society, the institutions of schooling cannot but be morally heterogeneous. But of course this does not mean an equal voice for all. As in social affairs generally, it is dominant groupings – white, male, middle class – whose professed morality is taken to represent the norm. The ways in which this moral dominance operates are more subtle and pervasive than the explicit teaching of lessons in sex education, for instance, or personal and social education. For, as this chapter has argued, the real moral teaching that goes on in schools takes place through their own institutional practices, their own unquestioned regimes. Opening up moral questions with young people, seriously debating the ethical dilemmas that we all face in our lives, can be done only within a classroom order that has itself been morally reworked. This means that teachers themselves have to abdicate the role of moral authority, to allow other, less familiar positions to be acknowledged in the classroom. This must entail maintaining every young person's right to speak without the threat of ridicule or intimidation. It may then be possible for children to explore their own problematic experience and to begin to engage personally with the huge complexity of human conduct.

9

Gender and the Curriculum

We generally think of pupils as a single category, and suppose that, in their formal schooling, girls and boys share much the same situation. By virtue of their pupil status, all young people apparently have access to an identical curriculum, and can in their later years make similar choices of options within it. There seems no reason in these circumstances for any particular pattern of divergence in educational performance between the two genders. Yet in fact there are consistent and widespread differences in the school achievements of girls and boys – differences that carry major significance for their future life chances.

The impact of gender on educational performance has for some time been a matter of concern for teachers and researchers. Until recently, this was seen as a question of differential overall attainment. Although girls generally did better than boys in all subjects during the early primary years, this pattern gradually reversed itself as schooling progressed, so that by the later secondary stage boys were markedly out-performing girls. But over recent years, the situation has changed. Both at primary and secondary levels, the imbalance currently favours girls, whose average school performance, overall, is consistently above that of boys.

At first sight, this situation seems to indicate that all is well – at least as far as girls are concerned. Previously problematic, female gender is now apparently no obstacle to educational progress. Yet closer attention shows that matters are not so simple, for – paradoxically – despite their generally higher attainment, girls remain persistently one down in the schooling system.

If on balance the achievement of female pupils outstrips that of their male classmates, their pattern of educational performance across the whole curriculum is far from equivalent. Girls persistently excel in English and languages, subjects in which boys regularly do badly. Conversely, boys do well in maths, science and technology. These differential 'abilities' markedly affect the choices pupils make, with few girls, for instance, opting for advanced levels of study in scientific or technological subjects.

For future life careers, these differences are far from incidental. Science-based employment, in engineering or industrial settings, is typically highly paid and of high status, as is work in advanced technology. In enabling access to these occupational spheres, success in school science and technology carries real material and social advantages; and this is recognised in the high prestige accorded to these subjects in the school curriculum hierarchy.

Over recent years major efforts have been made, with some success, to enable girls to enter and succeed in the traditionally masculine spheres of maths, science and technology. Many of these initiatives have involved an attention to the curricular materials involved in teaching: the texts, the worksheets, the activities. In science, for instance, these typically refer to male pioneers such as Newton or Darwin. Likewise, despite the fact that it was Marie Curie who first formulated the principles of radiation, one illustrated textbook in current use shows Henri Curie looking down a microscope, while his wife stands behind him, her hand on his shoulder. The implicit messages of such texts emphasise science as a masculine domain and exclude the possibility of significant female involvement. Similar messages are carried by the exemplification of scientific principles through reference to stereotypically masculine activities. In a secondary school lesson watched by Alison Kelly (1985), the phenomenon of eclipses is demonstrated using a football to represent the Earth. Had the teacher used a netball, or a balloon, suggests Kelly, the girls might not have sat there in total silence.

But the development of 'girl-friendly' curricular materials has meant more than a mere substitution of female for male pioneers of science, or the use of illustrations from prototypically feminine spheres of life. It has entailed, as far as possible, an attempt to reconstruct science itself as a subject for school study. The popular image of science as objective and impersonal, as concerned with *things* rather than *people*, is very much endorsed by the constitution·of school science. Physics and chemistry are characteristically taught and demonstrated as abstract principles, disconnected from the particular kinds of contexts to which they might apply; and this approach is one that girls in particular find alienating.

Patricia Murphy and Jannette Elwood (1997) describe an experiment in primary school science, in which the children work in pairs. This involves testing the time taken for sugar to dissolve in a cup of tea at different temperatures. In one pupil pair, the boy sets up a range of temperatures, beginning with cold. The girl objects, pointing out that nobody drinks cold tea, but the teacher tells the girl she is being difficult and overrules this objection. For such pupils, however, it is often precisely the human unreality of the task that makes science seem alien and pointless. Though to this girl's teacher the literal content of the task seems irrelevant, for the girl herself it holds crucial significance. As Karen Littleton remarks, 'Vehicles for task presentation are rarely, if ever, neutral in their effects . . .' The metaphors and images used in the presentation of the task can have an influence out of all proportion' (Littleton, 1997, p. 92).

That the surrounding meaning of a task can affect its performance is borne out by an experiment conducted some years ago by David Hargreaves (1983). He invited a group of primary age children to pass a narrow loop across a length of 'wiggly wire' without touching it at any point. If contact was made, a bell sounded. Half the sample were told this task was designed to assess how good they would be at mechanics and operating machinery. To the other half the task was introduced as testing their skill at needlework, sewing and knitting. For the two groups, the results were strikingly different, with boys excelling in the first condition and girls in the second. Children shine, it seems, on tasks that are the prerogative of their own gender.

An alternative approach to school science, which builds on this insight, has been developed by a group of Australian researchers (Hildebrand, 1996). This starts from the assumption that in physics, for instance, as in any other sphere, learning takes place through trying to make sense of problems that matter to people. So instead of the usual top-down, theory-led teaching, topics are introduced through pupils' own enquiries: about sun-block creams, for example, playground equipment, or bicycles. Genuine concerns about the social and environmental implications of science also tend to surface in the issue-based approach to chemistry pioneered by Janet Harding (1986). Here, discussion might start from questions about lead in petrol, acid rain, X-rays, or the design of household appliances.

Opening up the curriculum to real-life concerns make great demands on the knowledge and resources of already hard-pressed teachers – nor are such policies a panacea. Though these different forms of school science have been found to raise the performance, on average, of female pupils, this improved achievement is far from universal. Girl-friendly materials appeal, it seems, to many middle-class girls, but apparently do little to overcome the antipathy of working-class girls towards traditionally masculine subjects. Nor do those female pupils brave enough, and supported enough, to enter such male domains generally last long, tending to drop out of the advanced courses they have undertaken.

Ostensibly, girls and boys have equal access to school computers, both in formal study and in the informal usage of computer clubs, yet in practice male pupils hugely dominate these resources. This is true right from the start of children's encounters with this school resource. In the computer-based activities of some primary schools, boys regularly take control of the few machines available, leaving girls to look on. In free periods, again it is male pupils who secure exclusive access. One result is a general lack of female confidence, with many girls feeling they have fallen too far behind to make up lost ground in the future.

By the secondary stage, with its larger opportunities for this kind of work, just the same situation prevails. In a close study of eight secondary schools, Lynn Culley (1988) sat in on lessons in computer awareness. In the practical part of these lessons, as she witnessed, boys rush to take charge of the computers, elbowing girls out of the way, and often leaving them no access to a machine. Boys also dominate the discussion part of these lessons, asking more questions and making more comments; as a result they obtain a far larger share of the teacher's attention.

This pattern repeats itself in the more advanced computer

studies, where male exam entrants greatly outnumber female ones. In mixed classes for these studies, boys typically dominate the keyboard while girls look on. Where, rarely, the teacher insists on hands-on access for female pupils, this elicits considerable resentment. And again, by waving their hands and calling out, boys ensure that teachers attend to their needs rather than those of the quieter and more diffident girls. Not surprisingly, it is boys rather than girls who regularly participate in the optional activities of computer clubs. Girls who venture to enter this 'male territory' are typically made to feel uncomfortable and out of place.

All this cannot but result in very different attitudes towards computer technology. Though many girls pay lip service to the idea of equal female competence, their feelings about their own involvement are typically negative. Computers tend to be regarded, by both genders, as machines for boys and men, and as having a significant part to play in male, rather than female, adult lives and careers.

But school is not, of course, the first or only context in which the gender-differential meaning of computer use becomes established. The greater relevance of this technology for boys rather than girls is implicit in a hundred aspects of our social practice. We tend, however regretfully, to see as inevitable the crudely masculine character of computer games, with their war scenarios, and their physical, often violent, story lines. They are all, it seems, part of the world of boys. That world, equally naturally, includes a fascination with machines, with the workings of mechanical and electronic objects. Given this perception, most parents would not question the hours their son spends glued to the latest computer game, while their daughter talks with her friends or reads her books and magazines.

Talking and reading: the preferred activities of girls. It is not, perhaps, surprising that right from the start of schooling, female pupils outshine their male classmates in every aspect of language. In reading, in writing, in oral literacy, girls consistently do well. This success is maintained throughout their years of schooling, resulting in a level of exam success in English and other languages that is well above that of boys. And just as boys' superior competence in computer knowledge has its roots in out-of-school experience, encouraged by taken-for-granted perceptions of masculinity, so girls' communicative facility is integral with traditionally feminine social and personal pursuits.

This looks at first sight like a neat equation. Both boys and girls excel in educational spheres that are consonant with their conventional gender identity: boys in scientific–technological domains, girls in linguistic ones. It seems a balanced picture. But such is the unequal status of the two genders that female success, and the curriculum areas in which it manifests itself, become subtly downgraded.

As much research has shown, there is a double standard that applies to male and female school achievement. When boys do well in classwork, this is taken to signify real ability and personal flair. Yet the successes of girls are typically put down to diligence and hard work. Boys are thought to achieve educationally through innate brilliance, where girls manage to reach competence only through the conscientious following of rules. The same differential logic applies to failure; male pupils are lazy and uninterested; females ones are simply incompetent.

This perception is also reflected in the judgements of young people themselves. Not only do girls and boys alike tend to believe in the general superiority of male over female ability, but this assumption also governs their anticipations of their own future achievements – with boys overestimating, and girls underestimating, their actual attainment levels.

An interview with Valerie Walkerdine (1990) illustrates

this kind of differential judgement on the part of teachers. Faced with an equivalent level of attainment in a male and a female pupil, says a woman teacher, she would enter the boy, but not the girl, for a prestigious examination. The girl, she explains, is likely to have worked to the limit of her capacities, while the boy, who has probably achieved this level without effort, will do even better if he exerts himself to the full.

Of course such attitudes are not typical of all teachers, many of whom are acutely aware of female disadvantage and concerned to counter it in their own work. School culture, though, is inevitably shot through with influences from the wider social world; and one way in which these operate, within the educational system, is in systematically favouring the spheres of human life that are prototypically masculine.

In theory, all areas of the school curriculum have equal value. Science, technology and English should simply be viewed as alternative spheres of attainment. This is, however, not the case in reality. Where scientific and technological subjects have the highest prestige in the school hierarchy, English, by contrast, is seen as having only secondary importance. Academically able boys, for instance, are routinely expected to opt for maths, science or technology, rather than devoting themselves to studying English. There is a general consensus that this curriculum area holds only minor significance for male adult careers – probably the real touchstone in curriculum evaluation. The subject does not seriously count for boys, it is usually agreed; they need only a bare pass to get by in the future.

To many people, this argument would seem untenable. Surely in contemporary society, with its growing demands for literacy and communication skills, school English should be granted paramount importance? Yet this is to equate the forms of language that constitute the classroom subject with those demanded in the achievement of social power and influence in adult life.

Classroom forms of English, from the infant years on, favour the capacity for fantasy and imagination, and the development of self-reflective and empathic kinds of expression. These qualities are significant in both the language and the literacy sides of the subject. And they are qualities that mark the preferred reading and writing of girls throughout the schooling range: the fairy stories of early years; the personal dilemmas and love stories of pre-teen comics; the problem pages of teen-age magazines. As one girl remarks in a study conducted by the Assessment of Performance Unit (Gorman, 1988), 'I like reading things that help me understand my own and other people's problems'. The same social and humanistic interests characterise girls' writing, whether in voluminous letters to pen-friends or in narrative and descriptive school essays.

In general, boys read less than girls, but when they do, their preferred reading material is very different. According to the APU survey, by the age of eleven many boys are reading hobbyist magazines that relate, for instance, to stamp-collecting, cycling or model-making. By fifteen this preference is well established; boys choose books and magazines that 'give accurate information about how things work'. Nor is it only in its practical, informative content that boys' preferred reading material differs from girls'. In their language and styles of presentation, typically masculine forms of literacy are quite distinctive.

At the primary stage, both boys and girls read comics. As Janet White (1996) points out, comics for boys have a vocabulary all of their own. Whereas girls' comics use words with clear personal meaning, those aimed at young male readers adopt an obscure but authoritative-sounding language. In the typical science fiction world of these texts, boys encounter such words as blusteroids, the monad, gryznov, or shinobo. 'Such vocabulary', remarks White, 'however ludicrous to the adult eye, has a pedigree of scientism about it, and arguably plays its part in familiarising the young reader with a whole range of textbooks in which the vocabulary is similarly opaque but just as authoritative' (White, 1996, p. 99).

Comics for boys are also distinctive in the ways they tell their stories. Unlike the linear presentation of conventional narrative description, they characteristically employ complex visual formats, in which the story sequence is interrupted by explosive actions and stylized representations of sound effects. This kind of format does of course anticipate the graphics, tables and symbolic displays of computers; and in their self-directed writing, older boys characteristically adopt these forms.

Evidently the English situation is a complex one. Despite their acknowledged superiority in this area of the school curriculum, girls somehow end up being disadvantaged. This is partly because female achievement, and the spheres in which it prevails, come to be downgraded simply through their female character, but it is also because the kind of language and linguistic formats characteristically acquired by girls and boys differs in its social status and the access it allows to social power. For while humanistic and socially responsive skills may be at a premium in the English classroom, a facility with scientific and technocratic modes holds higher status in the wider world.

Schools are officially charged with social education. The National Curriculum defines its goals as 'preparing pupils for the responsibilities, opportunities and experiences of adult life', and 'promoting the moral and cultural development of pupils and society'. On these grounds alone, prevailing educational priorities clearly need to be challenged. For though the skills typically acquired by boys during their school years may provide access to individual advancement, it is the skills that girls characteristically develop that are likely to prove crucial in meeting the exigencies of social living. The responsibilities of adult life, the moral development of pupils and society: these objectives call for more than merely instrumental skills. If young people are to establish mutually satisfying personal relationships, let alone contribute to the public good, they will surely have to draw on such 'feminine' qualities as sensitivity to others' needs and the capacity for personal reflection.

Examination of English on the one hand, and computer studies on the other, shows that the meaning of any particular school subject is complex. The gendered significance of the curriculum derives not just from its explicit content, but, beyond this, from its links with young people's leisure activities, in an out-of-school world with its own clear expectations as to what boys and men, as against girls and women, should properly do. The realisation that countering female disadvantage is not merely a matter of changing curricular content has led a number of teachers to look more widely at the surrounding school context.

For many people concerned to promote girls' educational progress, the mixed groupings of the schooling system present an almost insuperable barrier. Whenever boys are taught alongside girls, they consistently monopolise the teacher's attention, and interrupt or ridicule any participation on the part of the girls. This picture is certainly borne out by a large-scale study of a number of comprehensive schools in Manchester, conducted by Madeleine Arnot and Gaby Weiner (1987).

These researchers sketch a typical first-year science lesson. The boys, as they witness, make a dash for the apparatus, and at once monopolise the more interesting activities on offer. They relish potentially dangerous situations – 'Great!' – acting with bravado towards the 'Do not' instructions that festoon the worksheets. The girls, meanwhile, react in timid and fearful ways towards the experiments, attracting much mockery from their male classmates. They hardly participate in class discusson, unlike the boys, whose use of technical terms is free and confident.

Such endemic problems, as many have seen it, will be overcome only by a segregation of the two genders. Single-sex education, by freeing girls from the constant put-downs of boys, may allow them to learn more confidently, at their own pace and in their own ways. Advocates of this approach point to the changes that often occur in girls-only teaching groups. Relieved of the inhibiting effects of male ridicule, girls become more outspoken, actively engaging with the teacher and taking chances in their questions and comments. These contexts also allow girls to work in their own preferred ways: discussing things together, and collaborating on learning tasks, as against the individualistic and competitive modes generally favoured by boys.

In practice, this form of education can at best be partial. Such single-sex schools as do exist stand outside the mainstream system, and, being privately funded, cater only for a selective intake. In the comprehensive sector, gender-segregation has been used as part of an equal opportunities programme within the particular curriculum areas associated with female disadvantage: those of maths, science and technology.

A large-scale initiative of this kind was entitled 'Girls into Science and Technology', and took place, again, in a number of comprehensive schools in Manchester (Murphy and Gipps, 1996). It entailed not merely separate teaching groups for girls in these school subjects, but the development of girl-friendly curricular materials, and an attention to raising awareness of gender issues on the part of pupils and teachers. That teachers themselves should need this kind of education, in the form of in-service courses, might seem strange. Yet, as the researchers found, it was often just their attitudes that tended to sabotage things, and may have accounted for the limited success of these initiatives. For some teaching staff involved in this work, for instance, such single-sex teaching discriminated unfairly against boys, a feeling reflected in the resentment of many boys at the "special" efforts being made for girls. For others, gender imbalances in attainment were seen as natural and inevitable.

Teachers, like the rest of us, form part of a society that systematically, and in a whole variety of ways, privileges its male members. It is only to be expected that those who work within the schooling system hold many of the differential assumptions and expectations applyimg to males and females. That this is so is evident in the different treatment routinely offered in school to girls and boys. At one end of the age scale, it is girls who are asked to help tidy up the infant classroom. At the other, most working-class girls, at least, are guided, in careers advice, into domestic, nursing or secretarial roles, often being 'cooled out' of vocationally more ambitious plans. This treatment relates, of course, to the general perception, in school as elsewhere, that – despite their currently poor performance intellectually – boys are innately superior.

Many attempts to counter male–female stereotyping in schools have viewed the role of women teachers as critical. If a traditionally masculine sphere of knowledge is taken over by a woman–teaching maths, for example – then surely pupils will come to revise their assumptions of female incompetence. Such women can in this way serve as role models for feminine achievement. It was just this situation that was examined by Rosie Walden and Valerie Walkerdine (1985), in a study that shows it to be far from simple.

These researchers sat in on the lessons of women maths teachers at both primary and secondary levels, and talked to them and their pupils about their classroom work. They found that the early years primary teachers felt generally confident in their teaching, which was associated with at least average attainment for both male and female pupils. But at the later primary stage, and still more at secondary level, matters were much less satisfactory. The teachers here were much less confident, and seemed unable to reverse the falling behind of their female pupils.

In school maths, the content of the curriculum changes markedly as schooling progresses: 'In early mathematics, domestic tasks (weighing, measuring, shopping) are used as a matter of course. This allows stereotypically feminine activities to be used as the site for the teaching of mathematics' (Walden and Walkerdine, 1985, p. 6). In this situation, not only is a female maths teacher likely to feel at home; she is seen by her pupils to have authority in the subject. The ideas and activities involved in her lessons relate to spheres the boys and girls expect her to know about, to be expert in. But as the subject advances, its content increasingly refers to the spheres of mechanics and engineering. And here, a woman's position is far more ambiguous. She must now speak about domains of experience with which she is probably unfamiliar, areas in which she feels something of a stranger. Even if she has managed to overcome such feelings, for her pupils her expertise is questionable. These are areas that do not belong to her as a woman, nor to the girls in her class: they are part of a domain that has been claimed by boys.

The complicated position of women maths teachers relates

also, as these researchers argue, to their place in the school's authority structure. School power, at secondary level, is characteristically male power. It is men who typically hold the more powerful job of caretaker, and women who work as cleaners. Male teachers greatly outnumber their female colleagues as heads and heads of department. In teaching maths, with its high school status, a woman teacher stands in an anomalous position. The authority bestowed by the subject is implicitly undermined by her own gender.

All this, as these researchers observed, has a profound effect on the way these women taught. In contrast with the general ease and confidence of those working in early primary education, women maths teachers in the secondary sector were typically ill-at-ease, diffident and uncertain of their role. This insecurity was particularly visible in their dealings with boys, towards whom, when challenged, they tended to be deferential. Of course something of this discomfort was inevitably communicated to their pupils, thereby reinforcing the very message their appointment was meant to counter. Implicitly it told girls: all this is not for us.

As this study suggests, altering female educational disadvantage is far from easy. Clearly, attention must be directed at the curriculum itself, which in scientific and technical areas all too often embodies stereotypically masculine content. But curricular initiatives alone will not be enough if they take no account of the whole surrounding school context. For in its authority structures and its established routines, school itself may act to contradict the would-be empowering messages of girl-friendly forms of learning. Above all, efforts to rework gender imbalances must engage with the whole culture of the school social world; and here, the problematic position of boys – the topic of the next chapter – holds key significance.

10

School Boys

'Girls may follow the same curriculum as boys,' writes
Michelle Stanworth, 'may sit side by side with boys in classes
taught by the same teachers – and yet emerge from school
with the implicit understanding that the world is a man's
world, (1981, p. 5). Despite strenuous efforts over the last
decade or so to eliminate the male bias of the education
system, boys continue to dominate school life. This is not, as
it once was, a question of superior masculine achievement.
As we have seen, girls now out-perform their male classmates
in almost every area of the curriculum, although, as noted in
the previous chapter, it is typically boys who excel in scientific and technological subjects through their monopolising
of classroom resources, and their numerical predominance in
these options.

But while differences in general academic performance no
longer favour boys, this does not mean that girls have now
gained an equal share of the educational cake. From her first
entry through the school gates to the day she leaves school, a
female pupil experiences a status that is essentially lesser.

Through classroom and playground encounters, in dealings with teachers and with fellow-pupils, she comes to learn that in the world of school her own importance is secondary.

How does this happen? How is it that, even with female-friendly teaching approaches, boys continue to push girls aside? Women science teachers, texts that foreground female achievement, collaborative methods of learning, unbiased careers advice, even courses for girls in assertiveness: none of these solutions have succeeded in equalising gender relations.

Compared with their female classmates, male pupils constitute a far more visible and salient presence. They are insistently *there*, demanding attention, impossible to ignore. To a large extent, this is a matter of 'trouble'. On every index of anti-school behaviour, boys overwhelmingly outnumber girls. Both truancy and exclusion from school are typically male preserves. Boys rather than girls constitute those officially defined as presenting emotional and behavioural difficulties beyond the resources of normal schooling.

Among boys who remain in school, many present disciplinary problems. In corridors or in the playground, bullying and harassment of girls are quite routine. Sexist behaviour also features in the constant disruption of classroom work: again, a typically male activity. For most teachers – especially women teachers – every lesson is likely to entail a barrage of male insolence, rudeness and inattention, a host of petty disruptive acts.

In situations such as these, it is hardly surprising that teachers' attention should be directed towards boys. Pupils who prove hard to control necessarily demand the energies of those in charge. In this way, despite teaching intentions, lessons are apt to become geared towards male rather than female pupils. This can happen even where teachers are committed to achieving a fairer share for girls.

As a teacher working for gender equality, Susan Tingle

describes her own struggles with a mixed group of secondary pupils. The work involved group discussion, followed by writing, about personally relevant topics:

> The boys plunge into things, interrupt discussion, can't keep still, can't wait. Ten boys in a class of twenty nine, they demand fifty per cent or more of my time. Yet the work they produce is often shallow, non-reflective, and is always messy . . . the boys, in protective groups, generally resist giving anything of themselves. They hide their feelings, they joke, they are loud, they are very physical (Tingle, 1985, p. 5).

The physical character of boys in school has been noted by many educational researchers. In routine classroom put-downs, boys react to girls' initiatives by fidgeting, sighing, tapping pencils, and so on. They shout. They commandeer space, appropriating not merely the territory of the playground, but that of the classroom too: leaning back in their chairs, spreading themselves out, restricting the movements of others. As Thomas Gordon (1992) put it, 'The physical school is a more spacious place for boys than for girls. For them, the school yard is larger, the corridors are wider, the classroom bigger, and the area surrounding their bodies greater . . . A boy who moves around the classroom, talks without putting his hand up, behaves "like a boy".'

Physicality is, in our culture, one of the defining features of masculinity. To be properly male involves a particular kind of embodiment: a large, muscular, athletic physique. Whereas early puberty in girls has complex and ambiguous significance, boys who mature early earn admiration from their peers. Male identity entails bodily power and control: being tough, aggressive, hard, active; and sport, as the sphere in which such qualities become developed, holds unequalled importance in the school world of boys. Competence in football defines a hierarchy of respect. Not merely does it exclude girls; it also demotes as 'feminised' those boys who lack the requisite physical skills. John Salisbury and David Jackson suggest:

> School sport doesn't just play a part in shaping boys' emotional and social lives. It also locks many boys into an aggressively virile culture. Through the masculinizing of their bodies . . . through constant tackling, kicking, throwing, yelling, jumping, running hard, boys tauten their muscles, put an arrogant hardness on their faces, throw out their chests and hold themselves firm and upright in an attempt to intimidate their opponents (Salisbury and Jackson, 1996, p. 208).

Being 'properly' boyish means acting hard and talking tough. Boys who fail, for one reason or another, to present this image come to be stigmatised as sissy and effeminate. This is the logic of a psychology of gender relations that, in polarising male and female, sees girls as weak, passive and dependent. It is a psychology widely held. Masculinity and femininity seem to denote opposites; and probably most people would subscribe to the view that human gender carries with it certain inborn traits. If male pupils are generally more boisterous, naughtier, more rebellious than their female classmates, this is only to be expected. Boys will be boys. Ruefully we shrug our shoulders, seeing boyish trouble as the price we must pay for the all-important dynamism, the competitiveness, the pioneering initiative of male character.

Men and women, boys and girls, are incontrovertibly different. At first sight, these differences can only be inbuilt, an intrinsic part of biological make-up. For they are, as many parents would insist, present right from the moment of birth.

Male babies are more active physically; female ones are less so, but more communicative. In toddlerhood, these differences become still clearer; small boys rush noisily around, while girls play quietly, in a smaller space, perhaps together. By the time they go to school, not only do children behave in highly gender-distinctive ways; they also typically segregate themselves in their own gender groups.

How can all this, so widely recognised, so apparently universal, *not* reflect the innate and inevitable concomitants of being born male or female? Surely gender differences are simply one, ineradicable, aspect of human nature? Yet, as many careful studies have begun to show, even infants in the earliest days of life are responsive to the expectations of those around them; and, for any parent, their baby's gender is far from incidental. Indeed, this is often a focus of concern even before birth. David Jackson recalls his mother telling him she had known he would be a boy because he had wriggled and kicked so hard during her pregnancy. She had commented approvingly on these early signs of masculinity: 'They called you "Bull" Jackson when you were in Paignton Hospital. You hollered and bawled so loud they could hear you right down the corridor' (Jackson, 1990, p. 146).

Several researchers have studied mothers in interaction with their infant children, using videotape records to look closely at what happens. Not merely do all mothers talk differently to boys and to girls. They also respond differently to the same behaviours, and accord that behaviour differential significance according to the baby's gender. Energetic physical activity is noticed and encouraged in male infants; vocalising and social responses, on the other hand, are welcomed in female infants. Thus, in their very first human encounters, babies experience treatment that is gender-differentiated. Through a multitude of subtle and intuitive communications, and long before such things could be put into words, they meet distinctive social expectations: what it means to be a boy or a girl.

This process continues as babies become toddlers. Where recordings have been made in nurseries and playgroups, these show that care-givers talk very differently to their male and female charges. In boys, robust activity is encouraged, with all its risks of destructiveness and minor injury. Violence, while not condoned, is seen as natural to masculine identity. 'Big', 'strong', 'tough' and 'brave' are terms of praise applied to male children, as showing proper manly enterprise and fortitude. In little girls, however, assertive or adventurous behaviour is discouraged; it carries connotations of being 'a proper little madam'. Approval is expressed, by contrast, for being 'pretty', 'sweet-natured' or 'neat and tidy'.

But it is school above all that teaches children – often in the harshest, most unmistakable terms – what is proper to their own gender, and what costs attach to its disregard. Through its regime, its institutional rules and practices, the schooling system accords its own official significance to the male or female character of its pupils. It is, however, the 'hidden curriculum', the habitual reactions, the routine talk of classroom, playground and staffroom, that convey most powerfully what it means to be a boy or a girl; and in these intricate and intuitively carried communications, it is the interactions between pupils themselves that hold the greatest force.

This is not to say that institutional features of schooling, and teachers themselves, do not play their part in the construction of their pupils' gendered identities. In virtually all secondary schools, for instance, the hierarchy is masculine: with men as head teachers and in senior management positions. Within curricular departments, at least those with high prestige, it is male teachers who typically hold responsibility. Decision-making, too, is apt to be in the hands of men. As

Susan Askew and Caroline Ross (1988) have found, ostensibly democratic staff meetings are characteristically biased towards male views, while the opinions of women teachers get disregarded.

More subtly, the organisation of schools, especially secondary schools, typically reflects and conveys traditionally male values rather than female ones. Authority and control are emphasised at the expense of caring personal relationship. Registers, assemblies, uniform: these features imply the unimportance of individuals, and an endorsement of relations of dominance and subordination.

The pastoral system – the place in school where pupils' personal feelings have an official place – is all too often merely an add-on. Within an institution whose values stand at variance with its own, this system, so far from making schools into caring and nurturing places, may even be used to discipline pupils. The same lack of institutional respect tends to be accorded to curricular spheres offering opportunities for personal kinds of classroom work. In personal and social education, for instance, young people may potentially reflect for themselves on social issues, on questions of value, on their own personal lives. Yet in many schools this subject is relegated to the most notoriously difficult times of day – the end of the morning, the very last period – if it is not actually forced off the timetable altogether.

In very obvious ways, the discipline system of schools carries messages about values; and characteristically, discipline at the secondary level is an authoritarian, macho affair. Power to define misbehaviour belongs to teachers, rather than being a matter of discussion and negotiation. Problems are treated as an individual offence, rather than the product of particular social dynamics. Concomitantly, penalties are imposed from above. School discipline makes no reference to the development of mutual respect, and a sense of social responsibility. On the contrary, it is seen as a question of authority, power and control on the one hand, obedience and conformity on the other.

Similar values operate in the way that many teachers, especially male teachers, see their own function. Their class-room persona is dominant, tough, aggressive. They teach from the front, allowing little pupil participation, shouting at any perceived infringement of classroom order. Such teachers see themselves as needing to maintain their own dominance by the exercise of sheer power. To be a properly strict teacher, in this perspective, involves the use of intimidation, with its implicit threat of violence.

One aspect of this attitude is its disrespect for 'soft' teachers. Because they are typically seen in these terms, women teachers in many schools are treated with hostility and contempt by their male colleagues. Not merely is their work undervalued and their opinions not taken seriously, but they are often treated with overt disrespect, even subject to 'playful' sexual harassment. Evaluated against male norms, women teachers are, unsurprisingly, found wanting. It is no wonder that many pupils echo such assessments, as in the case of a boy who told Mairtin Mac an Ghaill (1994), 'I would prefer a man in charge and most kids would. Even if you get a woman, she tries to act like a man. But the kids don't take her serious' (1994, p. 367).

If traditionally male values underpin many teaching philo-sophies, they have also increasingly come to dominate the ethos generally prevailing in schools. So far from embodying a respect for every pupil, a nurturing of caring and co-operative relationships, schooling has been forced into com-petitive and managerialist forms. A system that plays one school off against another also sets up its pupils in mutual competition. The ensuing educational hierarchy ensures that losers will outnumber winners. Such a traditionally masculine system, as Leonard Davies (1992) suggests, has been actively fostered by recent political movements: 'It is this version of masculinity – competitive, point-scoring, over-confident, sporting, career and status conscious – which has come to dominate school management. It articulates well with the overall themes of schooling, of hierarchy and individuation' (1992, p. 128).

All these features have a resonance in the ways in which male pupils define and live out their school identities. The common culture of masculinity is shared right across the school world, and finds expression in the comments of boys and teachers alike. On their side, male teachers may reprove 'silly' male pupils for 'acting like girls', or talk of a boy as 'hiding behind his mother's apron strings'. Such attitudes are clearly registered by those at the receiving end. As one boy remarks to Mairtin Mac an Ghaill, 'Like when we're changing after games, the teachers will say "come on girls, we haven't got time for you to put your make-up on"' (1994, p. 107). Or as another pupil describes: 'The men teachers are always on at us saying "don't forget to do your nails", or they show you up in front of your mates by saying "Has anyone see Hill's new dress?"' (1994, p. 107).

Such essentially abusive references to femininity typify dominant conceptions of male identity. Fundamental to these conceptions is a clear demarcation between male and female spheres, involving a contemptuous hostility towards girls and women. 'Proper' masculinity can be achieved only in opposition and superiority over what is feminine. Conversation among boys at school serves to claim such an identity, by sexist talk in which girls are portrayed as the objects of physical and sexual domination. Mairtin Mac an Ghaill describes what this means in the school he studied:

At Parnell School, one of the main functions of the young men's sex-talk was publicly to validate their masculinity to their male friends. This collective peer identity affirmation often manifested itself in terms of highly ritualistic obsessive discourses ... Their sexual narratives carried the predictable misogynous boasting and exaggeration of past heterosexual conquests and male heroic fantasies, in which women were represented as passive objects of male sexual urges, needs and desires. These male 'fictions' appeared to be crucial elements in setting the parameters of the prescriptive and proscriptive sex/gender boundaries that served to police schoolboys' performance by making them act like men (1994, p. 92).

Mairtin Mac an Ghaill refers here to policing; and, as many writers have described, the achievement of masculine identity is never secure. Closely observed, narrowly regulated by a watchful peer group, boys must continually monitor their own behaviour – continually perform, as Rob Pattman puts it (Pattman *et al.*, 1997). Any deviation from a macho role risks the ascription of effeminacy, with all its homophobic connotations. Desperate to belong to the 'male club', bidding for social acceptance and respect, boys must perpetually show themselves to be 'one of the lads': constantly engaged in bantering, swearing, verbal sparring, maintaining a tough, cocky and aggressive front.

For boys who are gay, the construction of masculinity as aggressively heterosexual entails exclusion and rejection. Except in those very few schools that have implemented firm anti-heterosexist policies, minority sexual orientations are likely to remain hidden as far as possible. But even for heterosexual boys, prototypical masculinity carries heavy personal costs. Not only is there a sense of a precariously achieved identity, the ever-present risk of being labelled 'sissy' or 'poofter', but a macho world is also a world with little tolerance for feelings: for the expression of affection and tenderness, for personal intimacy, for vulnerability. When physical contact, for instance, between boys themselves is highly suspect, any touch – unless it is a mock punch – is disallowed. In this situation, male peer groups are less a source of support than an eternally critical and potentially stigmatising audience. Those relations anticipate the male friendships of all too many adult men. Typically these centre not on shared confidences and mutual trust, but on some physical activity such as sport. Grounded in the perpetual fear of being found out to be 'not man enough', these friendships are characteristically shallow.

Several writers have portrayed, often poignantly, the loneliness and insecurity felt by boys who present, outwardly, a swaggering, boastful front. The two sides of school boyhood – the intimidatory and the vulnerable – are described in David Jackson's account of his own experience:

> We made constant jokes about 'browners' and 'queers' and were always on the lookout for any unguarded hint of effeminacy in each other's gestures and behaviour ... Any slight diffidence, stuttering oddness, weakness was seized upon by the rest of the group, held up for public inspection and devastatingly ridiculed (1990, p. 172).

Yet Jackson, himself a member of this persecutory group, also felt acutely vulnerable: 'The showers were the most terrifying places for "unmanly" boys like me. I used to position myself in the most secret corner of the changing room, protecting myself from being ogled or ridiculed' (1990, p. 179).

A macho image has anti-school connotations. Partly this is because the pupil role is felt to insult a 'hard man' identity.

For many boys, school work and conformity to teachers carries demeaning connotations of childishness. Being expected to sit quietly, obeying the teacher's instructions, seems to disrespect the maturity that many pupils claim, and to reduce them to the status of 'little kids'.

'I'll tell you something', remarks one boy to Mairtin Mac an Ghaill, 'when we came to this dump we believed in the three Rs, we were right little piss artists, right little plonkers. Well we learnt what schools were for, for keeping you down and bossing you about.' 'You see', adds another boy, 'the whole place is planned to boss you around.' And a third comments, 'The teachers think, I'm going to put this little sod down because he thinks he can rule the place' (1994, p. 58).

School as a battleground in which teachers and their male pupils struggle for dominance: it is a vision shared by many men teachers. And ironically, the more obviously this vision is lived out – in an inflexible school regime, harsh discipline, authoritarian classroom control – the more it is likely to provoke rebellion amongst male pupils. For all that boys in the classroom despise and decry 'softness' on the part of the teachers, their reaction to the assertion of school authority is a defiant one.

There is another aspect of classroom work that, in the perception of boys striving for an unchallengeably male identity, renders it unacceptable. Academic achievement is associated with girls. Whereas 'proper' boys muck about in lessons, so this perception portrays things, their female class-mates sit, docile and conscientious, doing what the teacher tells them. Even academically motivated boys find it neces-sary to dissociate themselves from the feminine associations of school work. They emphasise their choice of technical subjects, their interest in impersonal kinds of knowledge, in facts and figures, as distinct from anything involving social or emotional content. Writing about feelings – 'girls' stuff' – is contemptuously dismissed, as is the collaborative work of group discussion, particularly if it entails the sharing of personal experience. 'Real' work, boys' work, is defined in terms of something not remotely personal, as a product, and as individually produced.

A further, major barrier to positive engagement in academic work for many boys in school consists in its identification with mental, as against physical, experience. Classroom learning, in our schooling system, rigidly excludes bodily experience, and insists on a total suppression of physical activity during lesson time. This proceeds, of course, from a commonly held psychology that separates mind and body, and views learning as solely a matter of the intellect. One inevitable consequence of this questionable practice is the alienation of pupils for whom their physicality represents a central feature of their identity. Yet where teachers do invite pupils to perform physically – in drama, dance or expressive movement – this typically enhances the curriculum, and can transform classroom atmosphere.

If institutionalised learning has little place for bodily aspects of experience, its exclusion of social aspects is no less drastic. Classroom groupings ride roughshod over friendships and alliances. Apart from the pastoral system or in particular relationships with individual teachers, school pays little regard to pupils' family and community identities. In the curriculum there is scarcely a mention of contemporary social problems. Yet children and young people live in a complex social world, and have to make a place for themselves within it. Their own social position and relationships, their sense of acceptability and belonging, are issues of the utmost importance; and for many pupils, their particular social identity stands at variance with schooling, and is seemingly irreconcilable with academic success.

There is one constituency to which this situation applies with particular force: black boys. In school, black boys claim – and are generally accorded – a prototypical masculinity. Their reputed physical attributes are the object of envy and admiration among white boys. Out of school, they are 'heroes', as Tony Sewell (1997) puts it, 'of a street fashion and culture that dominates our inner cities'. This image is one of style and street-wise maturity: of cool hard-men who know how to handle themselves.

But the other side of the this macho identity is an antagonistic relationship with schooling: an antagonism felt on both sides. In non-attendance, many black boys vote with their feet. Out of all proportion to their numbers, they make up the majority of young people excluded from school. Their presence in the classroom is typically fraught with conflict; and confrontations with teachers tend to escalate rapidly into verbal or physical violence.

Yet despite this characteristically problematic relation with schooling, black boys actually value educational success. Far from being indifferent to academic achievement, they, like their parents, see exam credentials as the only reliable route to personal betterment in a racist society. If they generally reject the modes of classroom work that conventionally lead to academic attainment, this is because, as for many ultramasculine white boys, their perceived treatment as 'little kids' insults their manly status. They see their teachers as trying to show them up, to make them look small in front of their peers.

The general hostility between schools and their black male pupils is not merely one-sided, however. Black identity is viewed within the institutions of schooling as inherently problematic. In face-to-face encounters with black and white boys, teachers are apt to make differential interpretations. Behaviour seen as acceptable in a white pupil may be viewed as disruptive in a black one. The physical presence, the posture, the ways of walking adopted by young black males are all experienced by many teachers as insolent, even threatening.

These perceptions are underpinned by a view of black culture as fundamentally deficient. Without any real understanding of the nature and diversity of black social life, differences from dominant cultural forms are seen simply as deficit. This attitude, characteristic of the wider society, is one to which many teachers subscribe. Typically, it results in a gulf between schools and the black communities they serve. Some white parents – especially white middle-class parents – may maintain close contact with their children's schools. For most black parents, however, communication is generally infrequent and superficial. For some, contact occurs only when their child is about to be excluded; and at the hearings that form part of such proceedings, their concerns are often accorded little weight. Nor, with some honourable exceptions, do schools generally possess mechanisms for black parents to make a positive contribution. This accords with the prevailing view of black family life as essentially problematic and deficient.

For black pupils, as for any others, family and community membership are fundamental to their identities. In both overt and subtle ways, disrespect for black culture permeates the institutions of schooling. This means that black boys who strive for academic attainment face acute personal conflicts. As Tony Sewell describes (1997), a positive school orientation is seen as a betrayal of collective identity. In working at lessons, conforming to teachers, such pupils seem to be abandoning black culture. At least in the classroom, they must substitute Standard English for the patois of their mates. Seemingly co-opted by dominant social groups, they may feel compelled to dissociate themselves from distinctive black styles of hair, dress and music; and in embracing the individualism of a hierarchical academic system, they forgo the essentially collective ethos of their own community. No wonder, then, that for pupils such as these academic attainment carries, in Tony Sewell's phrase, a 'cultural sacrifice'.

If mutual hostility between schools and disaffected male pupils is to be overcome, both sides must make some accommodation. Ultimately, this means a reconstruction of masculinity itself. For it is the traditional understanding, in our society, of what it means to be male that acts to forestall possibilities of educational engagement for all too many boys. And if black boys seem to represent a particularly problematic group, this is at least in part because they stand as icons of extreme masculinity.

Schools themselves are, of course, deeply implicated in the reproduction of traditional assumptions about gender. In a multitude of direct and indirect ways, they teach young people a view of 'males on top'; and in this, the environment of the classroom and the playground mirrors the wider social world. In a school structure dominated by men, where policies reflect the views of male staff, where discipline is authoritarian, and where the curriculum of learning prioritises masculine stories, masculine concerns – in this kind of institutional context pupils learn unmistakable lessons about male power.

It is to aspects such as these that, more recently, those who work for gender equality in schools have paid attention. Earlier initiatives had focused on efforts to promote girls: to develop female-friendly materials and learning methods, to provide women role models, to offer girls assertiveness training. However, the assumptions underlying such approaches have, for many educationalists, come into question: it is girls who constitute the problem, they seem to imply. Help girls engage with school learning, encourage them to be more self-assertive in the classroom, and all will be well. This is an essentially compensatory strategy, rather than one that locates the problem in the fact of widespread and unquestioned male power.

In some pioneering schools, heads and teaching staff have begun closely to examine their own regimes and practices. This has entailed, at the level of institutional structure, an attempt to eliminate male bias in the relative status of staff at both teaching and ancillary levels.

Perhaps more importantly still, efforts have been made to rework the modes whereby school policies and disciplinary decisions are arrived at. As Tony Sewell (1997) has described, this sort of work calls for a democratising of school management. In particular, it demands the direct involvement of pupils themselves. Young people need mechanisms for tabling their own issues and concerns, and for debating the generally unacknowledged diversity of goals and values that bear on practices in school. Communication with the wider community is no less important, especially in the case of more educationally alienated groups.

In most schools, discipline is an adult preserve. It is teachers who generally decide, without reference to pupil views, what constitutes a misdemeanour, and what sanctions shall apply. Though many teachers interpret school rules with some leeway, others operate them in a highly inflexible way. This, as Sewell describes, makes for frequent potentially explosive encounters.

Personal appearance – a somewhat grey area in most schools – often constitutes an emotionally loaded sphere of teacher–pupil conflict. The omission of some item of uniform, the wearing of baseball caps or multi-coloured trainers: where one teacher may exercise tolerance, another may outlaw such practices, sometimes causing pupil outrage. Sewell instances a case where one particular teacher banned a black boy's haircut, arousing intense fury. This essentially 'petty' matter, as it seemed to the teacher, had actually cost the boy £40, and had involved a three-hour styling; but more importantly, it held symbolic currency, as a signifier of ethnic and cultural identity.

The way that teachers act in the classroom, how they relate to pupils, their typically differential treatment of boys and girls: all this conveys its own powerful messages. Given the moment-to-moment pressures of the classroom, the need to maintain control over an often unruly group of young people, it is impossible for teaching staff to stand back and reflect on their own behaviour. As David Jackson (1990) argues, this demands the time and space offered by in-service training. His own work has focused on developing an aware-ness of the different ways that as teachers, men and women talk.

In one of Jackson's courses, a group of men and women teachers went through a checklist of trends, identifying them as typically male or female. With 'a shock of recognition' on the part of male teachers, the whole group identified the following features as distinctively characteristic of men: hog-ging the show – talking too much, for too long; 'speaking in capital letters' – emphasising one's own opinions by body posture or tone of voice; transferring the focus of conversa-tion to one's own pet issues; restating what a woman has already said perfectly clearly; being condescending to women: – for example, 'now do the women have anything to add?' Debating all this amongst themselves, this group eventually arrived at certain agreed principles that should ideally govern the way people talk to each other in groups. These covered not merely the necessity for allowing everyone a fair share, not interrupting or putting other people down; it was also agreed that talk needed to be undogmatic, allowing the expression of doubt and uncertainty. Finally, group members emphasised the participative and co-operative functions of discussion, as against its typically male use for egoistic and competitive purposes.

Through work such as this, teachers can sometimes begin the difficult task of reworking taken-for-granted practices in school and classroom. An institutional context that does not in itself reflect macho values offers, at least potentially, opportunities for its pupils to behave differently. School rules drawn up with the participation of young people, a discipline system that allows some room for negotiation, teachers who treat girls and women teachers with respect: all this represents an implicit challenge to bully-boy culture. But if the deeply entrenched attitudes of sexism that pervade the wider society are to be reworked within the school context, boys themselves must play an active part.

For those who work on such tasks with male pupils, conflict forms a vital point of focus. Aggressive self-assertion and harassment of weaker pupils are fundamental planks of school masculinity. Their social meaning has to be explored and questioned. Playground fights, classroom incidents and flashpoints for personal and group hostilities must all come to be debated, mulled over. In systems of peer mediation, or in the context of personal and social education, boys are encouraged to work together to find non-violent strategies for resolving conflict.

But alternative behaviours can emerge from discussion only if pupils talk together in conventionally un-male ways. Like their adult counterparts, boys typically use group talk to interrupt each other, score points, and ride roughshod over contrary opinions. These ways of behaving have themselves to be made the focus of attention. This calls for male teachers who have worked on such issues in their own practice. Where such men command the respect of their male pupils, they can serve as role models. Their own preparedness to listen, to accept personal differences and treat every young person's opinion as worthy of attention: all this can help boys to begin to question their own habitual ways of relating to others. For, as has been said, schools are contexts where boys learn to be men; and male teachers who are looked up to can sometimes exercise a profound influence.

This kind of work is both difficult and delicate. Habitual ways of behaving are seldom accessible to conscious choice, and questioning them can seem to be questioning one's very identity: one's personal image and reputation, one's sense of belonging to a valued social and cultural group. For these reasons, as David Jackson (1990), among others, has insisted, such work in school can be undertaken only in a context of personal trust and safety. As the research of Sewell and Mac an Ghaill suggests, it calls essentially for male-only classrooms, and male teachers with rare qualities of sensitivity and insight. But, at least potentially, this unusual kind of school work offers large rewards, in freeing boys from a masculinity that, for them as for others, is costly and oppressive.

11

Schooling for the Future

Schooling is future-directed. Its rationale looks ahead, beyond today, to the adulthood of tomorrow. Preparation is the key word – 'preparation', as the National Curriculum puts it, 'for the responsibilities, opportunities and experiences of adult life' (1992, p. 3). In practice, adult life is equated with employment. In conventional thinking at least, the goals of education are defined as the certification of young people as possessing the knowledge and skills necessary for entry into the job market. It is in these terms that schools are implicitly evaluated.

Such assumptions, as suggested in the first chapter of this book, constitute a very narrow perspective on what education can mean. For young people themselves, the formal side of schooling represents only one part – and sometimes the least valued part – of their daily lives in school. For parents, too, social aspects of their children's experience in classrooms and playground are hardly immaterial. Indeed, these features may prove decisive in the preference for one school over another.

Quite apart from these considerations, the preparatory function of education does itself need to be critically questioned. In official rhetoric, schooling offers equal life chances to every pupil. Provided young people are prepared to work hard, they can, supposedly, equip themselves with the necessary credentials for success in the job market. This view sees opportunities as open to all. Its world is one of free individuals, each pursuing their own interests, preparing while young for a chosen future and, as adults, reaping the ensuing occupational benefits. In the hierarchies of academic attainment among young people, and of later employment status among men and women, ability and effort are thought to be all that matter.

Yet, as study after study has revealed, this picture is hard to square with reality. Inequalities emerge at even the earliest stages of schooling. Somehow, with depressing regularity, and despite the best efforts of teachers and parents, certain groups of children fall behind, and stay behind, in the race for academic qualification. And these are, of course, precisely those groups of children whose home backgrounds are marked by poverty, stigma and disadvantage.

From its first beginning, the schooling system is officially portrayed as a preparation for adulthood – particularly adult employability. Early numeracy and literacy enable children to begin to acquire the various types of knowledge which, in later secondary years, will constitute examinable subjects. It is on the basis of these certifiable forms of competence, we generally suppose, that potential employers select their personnel. On this rationale, the eleven years of compulsory education constitute a continuous path towards the goal of employability.

Put like this, it seems that every child who enters school has an equal chance of attaining necessary credentials. In reality, the conventional equation between certification and

employment ignores the brutal fact of continuing unemployment – there are not enough jobs to go round. But as argued
in previous chapters of his book, the schooling system is
weighted, in multiple and complex ways, towards the promotion of particular groups of pupils. The language of the
classroom and the content of its curriculum favour those
with 'cultural capital': children whose home backgrounds
embody dominant values. Such pupils inevitably emerge, in
the eyes of teachers and in formal tests of competence, as
possessing academic ability; and since being defined as 'able'
governs access to public examination, it is typically white
middle-class young people who end up better qualified than
those from working-class or minority cultural backgrounds.
And while girls do better at GCSE level, men get significantly
more first-class degrees than women – particularly at Oxford
and Cambridge universities.

If the whole schooling system is supposed to constitute a
cumulative progression towards certification, nevertheless
schools offer, in their last compulsory years, a specific form
of pre-vocational preparation. This involves the selection of
options: particular school courses, some leading to national
examination, some not. On the face of it, this feature, again,
offers every pupil an equal chance of selecting their own best
vocational choices, but in practice the same factors operate,
in subtle ways, to privilege certain groups over others.

Being a girl, as has already been argued, means being
disadvantaged in schooling, and this disadvantage continues
into the final, vocationally focused stage of education. Over
a decade ago, Theresa Grafton and her colleagues (1987)
made a study of the examinable courses being offered to
male and female pupils. The curent situation was one of
widespread unemployment. In this economic context,
teacher–advisers, like most people in the wider society, were
particularly concerned about the role of young men: 'the

proper breadwinners in the family', as they were generally seen. It was boys, therefore, whom they guided into occupationally relevant training courses. Girls, on the other hand, were to be prepared for an essentially domestic future role. Female work was seen as secondary. Rather than vying with young men for scarce employment openings, they were to be groomed, through courses such as education for parenthood, to be wives, mothers, home-makers.

In the years since that study was carried out, much has altered. With economic changes in employment, jobs, especially in the growing service sector, are no longer a male preserve. Traditional attitudes towards the role of women in society have come under vigorous attack, and there are now at least some legal safeguards of female employment rights. Yet gender stereotypes die hard. In the option system that schools offer, young women still remain disadvantaged.

Within the context of one closely studied school, Mairtin Mac an Ghaill (1994) traces the differential occupational destinies of male and female pupils. As he suggests, recent educational changes have made for a new kind of hierarchy in secondary school careers. Traditionally, this has been a matter of the superiority of academic kinds of course, as against low-level 'vocational' preparation; but with the pressures on schools to make classroom learning maximally relevant to employers, the curriculum at secondary level has become increasingly vocationalised. This movement has been intensified by the growing numbers of business sponsorships in schools of facilities such as those of information technology.

This does not mean that, for a minority of pupils, an academic school career does not still exist. Certainly, for an elite group of middle-class young people, this remains viable. Their options, at GCSE and A-levels, are those they will take further at higher educational institutions. But for most pupils vocational rather than academic learning is now increasingly the norm in the final stage of schooling, and this form of learning has its own grading system. The new hierarchy, argues Mac an Ghaill, accords its highest status to the most technologically advanced spheres of the vocational curriculum. As against low-level, practical skills, it is the areas of technology, computer studies and business studies that hold real prestige; and, characteristically, these subjects have become masculinised. Overwhelmingly, they are taught by male teachers, and male students greatly outnumber female ones.

Where young men are typically encouraged into high-tech and commercially relevant courses, young women – at least those from working-class backgrounds – are subtly channelled into low-status kinds of training. Their paid employment, it is still generally supposed, will be of essentially lesser importance than that of men. Its secondary character is underlined by the courses that will prepare them for an ancillary role: typing, office skills, and personal presentation. But since in most schools motherhood is envisaged as their real career, working-class girls are characteristically guided into courses in child care.

'A lot of these girls,' remarks a male teacher to Mac an Ghaill, 'the ones in low sets, they will be married at a young age, and they need to have the appropriate skills to cope.' His colleague, another male teacher, disputes the assumption of marriage: 'Well, let's be honest, a lot of them aren't even going to get married. So it's even more important we train them for parenthood, isn't it?' 'These girls lack confidence,' proclaims a third male teacher. 'A lot of them have problem backgrounds. They will tell you the care courses we have devised for them gave them back that confidence. It tells them they can be as good as any of the high-fliers here. The new vocational courses have given them new skills and, most importantly, confidence in themselves that comes from acquiring those skills.' But this claim is scarcely borne out by the bitter comments of a young woman at the receiving end: 'The teachers told us to write down what we had learned from the caring course. I told him nothing. And then he said what about all the stuff you learned about child care. What a stupid man. I couldn't even begin to tell him, that's not learning. I do all that at home. I have to look after my younger brother and sister' (Mac an Ghaill, 1994, p. 119).

Most schools also offer directly vocational guidance in the form of the careers advice available to school leavers. The advice offered by the school's Careers Service is supposed to be neutral and non-directive. Following the advisory interview, an Action Plan, agreed by the young person, is produced. Yet here again subtle pressures may operate to guide different groups of pupils into differentiated occupational destinies. Two young people may possess exactly the same pattern of GCSE results, but gender, class and ethnicity are likely to govern the kind of guidance they receive. Just as young women may be implicitly discouraged from aiming high, so working-class and black young people will be 'cooled out' from career choices that seem to their adviser to be over-ambitious.

The assumptions underlying this kind of differential treatment are unlikely to be conscious; instead, they proceed from a failure to envisage a world other than the current status quo. When a young black woman declares her intention to become a barrister, the careers adviser feels a sense of incongruity. A black barrister, a black female barrister? It seems wildly improbable. For her own sake, the girl must be redirected, must be helped to make a more 'realistic' choice.

Of course such reasoning is only too obviously endorsed by contemporary social actualities. Oxbridge, the golden road to high-status work, is the preserve of an elite public school constituency. Though representing only 7 per cent of the population, this group, at last count in 1997, held 46 per cent of available places. At the other end of the social scale, very few black and working-class people hold top jobs, and women are grossly under-represented in senior positions. But for many, their situation is not merely one of low-status, poorly paid work. The effects of economic recession, the lack of long-term investment and the withdrawal of welfare benefits are felt, disproportionately, by the most disadvantaged groups. Unemployment in 1994, as the Runnymede Trust (1994) documents, affected 16 per cent of white people, 31 per cent of Pakistani/Bangladeshi people, and 47 per cent of black people – all having comparable levels of educational qualifications.

Young people themselves are typically well aware of the insecurity of the job market. Conscious of the likelihood of short-term work and serial unemployment, of the apparent need to obtain credentials, many more pupils than before now opt to stay on beyond the statutory leaving age. And for a young person at this point, there is, ostensibly, a plethora of choice amongst the educational and training courses, and the work experience placements available to them.

In a large-scale study of sixteen-year-olds in south London at this point of transition, Sheila Macrae and her colleagues (1997) are tracing the paths taken by particular groups of young people. One focus is the impact of guidance offered by various professional advisers: careers counsellors, tutors in schools and colleges, Job Centre staff, youth and community workers, and employers themselves. As these researchers have found, subtle pressures operate, in these forms of guidance, to separate sheep from goats: to channel different social and cultural groupings into different vocational destinies.

One major divide, in the field of post-sixteen education, is that between school sixth forms, on the one hand, and further education colleges on the other. These two kinds of institutions overlap in terms of the courses both offer; and both are apparently equally open to all students. In fact, as Macrae documents, the fierce competitiveness imposed on tertiary, as on secondary schooling, makes for desperate tactics to recruit. To survive as institutions, sixth form colleges and further education colleges must vie with each other and other institutions to attract student numbers. Here is a senior college manager admitting one such strategy: 'It probably isn't in schools' interests to educate pupils too well about the various options at 16. They want to hold on to the students, so I'd guess they tell them about the courses they have on offer and that's it' (MacLeod, 1997).

Needless to say, such practices are unlikely to further students' interests, but in a context where financial viability is all-important, other considerations take priority. In the words of a college student counsellor:

> I suppose it could be argued that it is a bit of a con piling students into these courses that probably won't lead directly to employment, but if we don't put them on, others will, and the students will take their money elsewhere. Money, of course, rules, and as students mean money, we supply, or try to supply, them with what they want. We follow the fashion to stay in business and hold on to our jobs.

Strategies such as these can include taking on young people for courses they are very unlikely to complete, and then, when they fail or drop out, encouraging them to transfer to a further course.

In this dog-eat-dog context, it is the academically better-resourced sixth form colleges that typically win out in attracting highly motivated students, who are overwhelmingly white and middle class. The intake of further education colleges, by contrast, is typically of working-class and black students, and those with poor disciplinary records. Inevitably, as Stephen Ball (Ball *et al.*, 1997b) remarks, this situation is one of niche marketing. With the resulting segregation by race and class, possibilities of choice, for students themselves, are unevenly distributed across the market.

Within the ethos of open choice across the market of post-sixteen education, young people find themselves targeted, in subtle ways, according to their particular social identity. The processes involved are generally indirect. Every educational institution now has to market itself to meet the pressures to keep up numbers; as Ball and his colleagues describe, schools and colleges are highly image-conscious, and often spend lavish resources on promoting themselves. If they are to remain institutionally viable, they must compete with others. Concerned to attract certain kinds of student and to deter less appropriate ones, a college brochure may feature photographs that highlight particular young people and particular lifestyles. 'People like you come here', the subtext urges the hoped-for intake, 'you'll find yourself at home in this environment'.

In the context of educational and training alternatives, how do young people make their choices? How influenced are they by the professional advice offered to them? In the findings of this research project, the decisions of young people themselves are based far more on grapevine knowledge than on any official guidance. Hearsay, rumour, word-of-mouth: these weigh heavily in the balance against what a formal adviser may say. Compared with the information offered in school or college brochures, the suggestions of parents, siblings and, above all, friends carry conviction. And, perhaps unsurprisingly, personal impressions are often paramount:

The journey to the college, its location, its physical condition, the lay-out, size and lighting in the rooms, graffiti, litter, even the smells within the building all carried important messages that could tempt or turn-off a prospective student. On these grounds alone a college could be declared 'alright' (meaning 'good') or 'rubbish' (Macrae *et al.*, 1997, p. 5).

Given the marked segregation of colleges by class and 'race', it is hardly surprising that such features loom large in students' reactions. As one young woman, hoping to make a new beginning, remarks to Macrae:

It is all rough people go to that college. I want to go to a nice smart college where I can just learn, without getting hassled or talked to, I just want to go there, do my work, go home and relax. It's all rough shabby people who don't want to do no work, they just go there and hang around. I've done enough of that, I need to learn and I want to go to a smart College where I don't know nobody so nobody can drag me in give me hassle and stop me learning because if I went there I might be just like them and not go to lessons and that. That is too many shabby Black boys go to that one anyway (Macrae *et al.*, 1997, p. 6),

Going to one college rather than another, or choosing a particular training course over an alternative one, can have long-term occupational consequences. On the face of it, decisions made on the basis of hearsay, or of personal first impressions, seem arbitrary. How an institution looks at first sight, or emerges from the experience of a friend-of-a-friend: surely these cannot compare with the advice of an experienced, knowledgeable professional? Even a student who has actually attended the college in question can know only about the particular course he or she has taken there. An official adviser, on the other hand, is widely informed about all the courses of study available, and how they may differ across particular institutions.

Students do in fact often make choices that are academically ill-informed. The young people being studied by Macrae and her colleagues include some who end up on unsuitable courses. But this does not mean that choosing options on purely academic grounds would be better. Colleges and training placements, like schools themselves, are social contexts; and just as children need to fit in comfortably with their peers at school, their chosen post-school setting has to be one where they can feel at home. In these personally vital terms the first-hand experience of a mate, or one's own intuitive sense of the place, must constitute a sounder guide than the advice of someone who is felt, perhaps, to be distant from oneself, and who knows the institutions concerned from a quite different position.

A more fundamental issue is that of the relation between school and post-school training, on the one hand, and employment on the other. Our education system is predicated on the assumption of a close connection. Schooling leads naturally and inevitably, so we think, into the world of work. The better qualified young people are, the greater access they will secure to better paid and higher-status jobs.

But this equation is a highly dubious one. This is not only because comparable certification does not guarantee comparable job opportunities; differences in gender, 'race' and class still ensure differential treatment. It is also the case that access to work openings is itself governed by the functioning of social networks. In many of the most powerful positions in society – those of medicine or the law, for instance – the 'old boy network' is well known. This acts informally to ensure that such posts will be open only to people who inhabit similar social worlds and share the same, culturally dominant, values. For the far less prestigious jobs available to working-class people, a comparable social filter exists. Getting work in the building trade, for instance, is typically mediated by personal contact. For many jobs, having a friend or family member already there is what counts, rather than the production of any educational qualification or training certificate.

'I know what I need to know from the streets,' remarks one boy to Tony Sewell (1997). Many young people already know much more than their teacher–advisers about state provision and their own local economy. Some school leavers reject altogether the official rhetoric about the relevance of certification. This is particularly the case for those whose 'race' or social class tend to debar them from desirable kinds of work. Black young men, for instance, often see no link between schooling and employment. Some few, bypassing the usual routes, may succeed in setting themselves up as entrepreneurs. This happened in one case described by Sewell. While still at school, a young black man had already established a business as a barber, carrying his mobile phone into the classroom to make appointments with his customers.

The relation between schooling and occupational destiny is evidently not straightforward. But for most people, education should be more than a mere servicing of the labour market; and preparation for adult life should go beyond a merely instrumental function, a delivery of employable skills. The National Curriculum uses the phrase 'The responsibilities, opportunities and experiences of adult life'; surely these go well beyond paid work? Many young people, and those who care about them, look to schools to educate their pupils, in some sense, for the roles they will take as adults in society.

Most secondary schools do attempt to provide, for their older pupils, some form of preparation for adult life, but this is typically patchwork, narrowly defined, and tailored differentially for different pupil groups. Courses in preparation for parenthood, for instance, are generally offered to girls alone. This kind of education is seen as inappropriate for boys even though most boys will also become parents. The questionable assumption underlying this practice is that bringing up children is solely a woman's responsibility.

The content of such courses is, in any case, open to criticism. It embodies ideas about infancy, early childhood and motherhood that would be challenged by those now working as developmental psychologists. Nor does this kind of training build on the existing first-hand knowledge of many of its recipients. Instead, as the girl previously quoted remarks with some bitterness, it assumes its students to be totally ignorant of the realities of child care.

If the parental role is viewed as a female preserve, social education in school is aimed at all young people. What is entailed in this sphere of learning, as Simon Bradford (1997) describes, has undergone considerable change over the last forty or so years. During the 1960s, within a broadly liberal ethos, it was understood to mean the development of social responsibility, conceived as a balance between personal autonomy and self-regulation. Young people were to be helped to understand personal and social relationships, and the impact on these of sexuality, race and gender.

In the more radical movements of the 1970s and 1980s, Bradford suggests, ideas about empowerment came to dominate this area of education. Young people were to be encouraged to think about the social forces to which they and others are subject: poverty, unemployment, racism, sexism, disablement. Their education in such ideas was not to be merely academic, but enabling. Rather than being victims, young people were to become active social agents in their own lives.

The ideas that Bradford describes certainly made an impact beyond schooling. The Children Act of 1989 surely embodies a respect for the social agency of even the youngest child. In schooling itself, similar principles can be seen to underlie the definition of education for citizenship in the National Curriculum. This document declares: 'Learning about duties, responsibilities and rights is central to this component. Rights include civil, political, and social and human rights and how these may be violated by various forms of injustice, inequality and discrimination, including sexism and racism' (1990, p. 6).

To implement such principles fully in schooling would mean a radical reworking of the whole curriculum. As things are, however, social education can only constitute an add-on subject, which inevitably stands at odds with much of its surrounding context. This is more the case for some versions of the subject than for others. In its more traditional forms, social education is defined as social and life skills. Young people are offered training in acquiring inter-personal competences. Skill in presenting onself to best advantage, in managing social encounters without awkwardness, will, it is assumed, enable young men and women to make their way in the world. Assertiveness training, or courses in communicative competence, are based on this kind of rationale.

A philosophy such as this essentially divorces social relationships from their particular contexts, and makes them a matter of individual personal attributes. In this, it omits any consideration of power. A job interview, for instance, is viewed as a simple meeting between two individuals, each with their own personal characteristics. Techniques of impression management appear, in this perspective, to be no more than desirable additions to the applicant's personality. Yet for many young people, the obligation, inherent in the situation, to conform to alien codes of dress, style and ways of speaking carries deep resentment. This feeling must of course be suppressed in order not to sabotage personal marketability, for the context is not merely one of personal communication between two individuals, each with their own particular personality. Rather, it is an encounter between two people with very different levels of social power. To conceal these structural inequalities is, as Phil Cohen puts it, to present the selling of labour as though it were a free exchange: 'class subjection is thus represented as its opposite – a position of individual mastery' (Cohen, 1997a, p. 290).

Power in society is associated with what has been called cultural capital. For the psychologist David Smail (1993), this entails an understanding of the more remote means – the 'distal' rather than the 'proximal' powers – that ultimately control social functioning. This understanding derives from a position with personal access to means and resources whereby distal influence works:

> The typical middle-class person, for example, occupies a world of powers and opportunities much less available to the average working-class person – indeed the difference in their availability is partly definitive of class. The manager is trained for and inducted into a world where (relatively) distal powers are mediated linguistically and procedurally by means largely unavailable to the worker . . . When Mrs Wright, a highly respectable and socially conscientious woman, finally succumbed to despair at the damp and generally sordid condition of her council house, she ended up abusing the housing manager down the telephone and threatened him with a duffing up by her two large sons. The world of pithy letter writing and veiled hints about personal access to MPs, public health departments, etc – the paraphernalia of association with power – was completely beyond her ken, and all she achieved by her phone call

was a menacing visit from a council minion who frightened her into continuing to suffer in silence (Smail, 1993, p. 40).

Smail's example concerns the lack of a certain kind of cultural capital on the part of one particular working-class woman: her lack of access to the means and resources that constitute the mechanisms of social power. Can education change this? The high principles that inspire statements about education for citizenship call, implicitly, for a redistribution of cultural capital, and the enfranchising of presently disenfranchised groups. Traditional social- and life-skills courses seem unlikely to achieve any such goals. Individualistically conceived, they rest essentially on an acceptance of the current social status quo.

Some recent school projects have, however, developed a very different approach to this area of education. Typically located within the sphere of cultural studies, they seek actively to develop young people's political literacy. This is partly a matter of promoting a sophistication towards the mass media. Communications are carefully scrutinised to reveal their hidden agenda: the ideological messages they imply. This kind of activity is certainly not a new one for adolescent girls and boys. Most young people, so far from being naïve recipients of propaganda, are critical and often cynical towards what is offered on their television screens. Rather than creating new capacities, these kinds of courses essentially enhance existing ones.

Text analysis and critique, the deconstruction of media messages: these have traditionally been purely intellectual tasks. From an essentially neutral standpoint, unaffected by any particular values, the critic examines the biases and unstated assumptions hidden within the chosen material. For young people about to leave school for the arenas of adult life, such an exercise would be arid indeed. In the much more promising work of Phil Cohen and others, cultural studies becomes applied cultural studies: the material at issue is examined in the contexts of young people's own lives.

Cohen's project, 'No Kidding', has already been briefly described in the context of school knowledge. What needs emphasising here is its significance in enabling young people actively to challenge conventional accounts, for in this project major disjunctions emerge between official advice and material about the transition from school and their own first-hand experience. In group visits to work sites, these school leavers closely question those involved, not as detached observers, but out of a need to know. Discrepancies between managers' and workers' accounts, social atmosphere, unofficial job benefits: these aspects, in spoken form and on photographic record, form the focus of later discussion. Rather than official careers brochures, the material of possible employment pathways becomes created by the young people themselves. Alive for them, it allows them to consider their own future possibilities and predicaments. They argue about the position of women workers, the exploitation of many trainees, the relative advantages and disadvantages of working in small businesses or co-operatives.

More broadly, however, this kind of work directly engages these young men and women in what can only be defined as political debate. From discussing their own possible futures, they progress to broader questions: the routine sexism of working life, managerial discipline and resistance, who controls the labour process, the place of the hidden economy. Spontaneous rather than teacher-scripted, these debates link the personal with the political.

Educational projects such as Cohen's are, of course exceptional, depending as they do on special research funds and staff with special types of expertise. For most secondary schools no such resources are available. Education for citizenship, as defined by the National Curriculum Council, typically remains the ideal rather than the reality of classroom work. Because these principles, unlike those of the core curriculum, have no statutory force, it is open to individual schools to adopt or ignore them. And as Ken Fogelman (1996) argues, in the context of an already overcrowded curriculum, teachers must make strenuous efforts if they are to include anything significant within this sphere of education.

In their daily work, teaching staff face timetabling pressures that make it difficult to build in non-obligatory kinds of learning. Yet despite this, many teachers remain committed to this kind of education. As one survey of secondary schooling shows (Whitty *et al.*, 1994), there is widespread support among teachers for themes such as these, which essentially cut across the curriculum rather than belonging within one particular subject area. Inevitably, actual practice lags behind hoped-for purposes. However, as another study (Fogelman, 1991) finds, the community-related activities in which most schools now involve their fifteen- to sixteen-year-old pupils can potentially mediate citizenship: the development of the capacity for responsible participation in society.

Our present schooling system makes it hard for teachers to address, together with young people, the real issues and dilemmas that will face them as adults living in our society. For this is impossible without personal engagement on the part of learners, and mutual trust and respect between learners and teachers. It is just these qualities, in classroom relationships, that the institutional organisation of learning makes so hard to achieve. Yet, where dedicated teaching staff find corners in the system, links can sometimes be made between classroom work and life beyond. Through learning ventures that embrace real issues, young people may come to develop a capacity for reflection, a space that allows some sense of owning their own lives.

References

Adams, E. and Burgess, T. (1992) 'Recording Achievement', in Berlak, H. *et al.* (eds), *Towards a New Science of Educational Testing and Achievement*, Albany, New York Press.

Ariès, P. (1962) *Centuries of Childhood*, London, Cape.

Arnot, M. and Weiner, G. (eds) (1987) *Gender and the Politics of Schooling*, Milton Keynes, Open University Press.

Askew, S. and Ross, C. (1988) *Boys Don't Cry: Boys and Sexism in Education*, Milton Keynes, Open University Press.

Ball, S. (1987) *The Micro-Politics of the School: Towards a Theory of School Organisation*, London, Methuen.

Ball, S.J., Maguire, M. and Macrae, S. (1997a) 'The Post-16 Education Market: Ethics, Interests and Survival', Paper to Annual Conference, British Educational Research Association, University of York.

Ball, S.J., Maguire, M. and Macrae, S. (1997b) 'Race, Space and the Further Education Market', Paper to Annual Conference, British Educational Research Association, University of York.

Barnes, D. (1986) 'Language in the Secondary Classroom', in Barnes, D., Britton, J. and Torbe, M., *Language, the Learner and the School,* Harmondsworth, Penguin.

Baur, M. (1981) 'Social Interaction in Primary School Classrooms: The Perceptions and Experience of Teachers and Pupils', unpublished PhD thesis, University of London.

Billig, M. (1987) *Arguing and Thinking*, Cambridge, Cambridge University Press.

Blishen, E. (1969) *The School that I'd Like*, Harmondsworth, Penguin.

Bourne, J. and Cameron, D. (1996) 'Disciplining English: The constitution of a national subject' in Woods, P. (ed) *Contemporary Issues in Teaching and Learning*, London, Routledge.

Bradford, S. (1997) 'The Management of Growing Up: Youthwork in Community Settings, in Roche, J. and Tucker, S. (eds), *Youth in Society*, London, Sage.

Broadfoot, P. (1979) *Assessment, Schools and Society*, London, Methuen.

Brown, G., Anderson, A., Shillcock, R. and Yule, G. (1984) *Teaching Talk: Strategies for Production and Assessment*, Cambridge, Cambridge University Press.

Brown, S., Riddell, S. and Duffield, J. (1996), 'Responding to Pressures: A Study of Four Secondary Schools, in Woods, P. (ed.), *Contemporary Issues in Teaching and Learning*, London and New York, Routledge.

Bruner, J. (1996) *The Culture of Education*, Cambridge, Mass., and London, Harvard University Press.

Burman, E. (1994) *Deconstructing Developmental Psychology*, London and New York, Routledge.

Cohen, P. (1989) *Really Useful Knowledge: Photography*

and Cultural Studies in the Transition from School, Stoke-on-Trent, Trentham Books.

Cohen, P. (1997a) *Rethinking the Youth Question: Education, Labour and Cultural Studies*, Basingstoke, Macmillan.

Cohen, P. (1997b) *Forbidden Games: Race, Gender and Class Conflicts in Playground Culture*, Dagenham, Centre for New Ethnicities Research, University of East London.

Craib, I. (1988) 'The Personal and Political', *Radical Philosophy*, no. 48, 14–15.

Culley, L. (1988) 'Girls, Boys and Computers', *Educational Studies*, no. 14, 3–8.

Davies, L. (1992) 'School Power Cultures under Economic Restraint', *Educational Review*, no. 43 (2), 127–36.

Department of Education and Science (1977) *Language: The Bullock Report*, London, HMSO.

Department of Education and Science (1992) *The National Curriculum*, London, HMSO.

Donaldson, M. (1978) *Children's Minds*, London, Fontana.

Epstein, D. (1993) *Changing Classroom Cultures: Anti-Rac,ism, Politics and Schools*, Stoke-on-Trent, Trentham Books.

Fogelman, K. (1991) *Citizenship in Schools*, London, David Fulton.

Fogelman, K. (1996) 'Citizenship Education in England', in Kennedy, K. (ed.), *Citizenship Education and the Modern State*, Reading, Falmer Press.

Gipps, C. and Murphy, P. (1994) *A Fair Test? Assessment, Achievement and Equity*, Milton Keynes, Open University Press.

Goddard-Spear, M. (1983) 'Sex Bias in Teachers' Ratings of Work', Paper at GASAT Annual Conference, Oslo.

Gordon, T. (1992) 'Citizens and Others: Gender, Democracy

and Education', *Studies in the Sociology of Education*, no. 2 (1), 43–55.

Gorman, T.P., White, J., Brookes, G., MacLure, M. and Kispal, A. (1985) *Language Performance in Schools: A Review of APU Language Monitoring, 1979–1983*, London, HMSO.

Grafton, T. *et al.* (1987) 'Gender and Curriculum Choice', in Arnot, M. and Weiner, G. (eds), *Gender and the Politics of Schooling*, Milton Keynes, Open University Press.

Gray, J. and Wilcox, B. (1996) 'The Challenge of Turning Round Ineffective Schools', in Woods, P. (ed.), *Contemporary Issues in Teaching and Learning*, London and New York, Routledge.

Harding, J. (1986) *Foundation Chemistry Course from Issues*, McClintock Memos no. 5, 1–9.

Hargreaves, A. (1994) *Changing Teachers, Changing Times*, London, Cassell.

Hargreaves, A., Earl, L. and Ryan, J. (1996) *Schooling for Change: Reinventing Education for Early Adolescents*, London and Washington, Falmer Press.

Hargreaves, D. (1983) 'Tasks and Gender-typing', *New Society*, 10 March.

Hargreaves, D. H. (1975) *Deviance in Classrooms*, London, Routledge & Kegan Paul.

Hartley, R. (1986) 'Imagine You're Clever', *Journal of Child Psychology and Psychiatry*, no. 27 (3) 383–98.

Highfield Junior School (1997) *Changing our School: Promoting Positive Behaviour*, London, Institute of Education.

Hildebrand, G. (1996) 'Redefining Achievement', in Murphy, P.F. and Gipps, C.V., *Equity in the Classroom: Towards Effective Education for Girls and Boys*, London and Washington, Falmer Press.

Jackson, D. (1990) *Unmasking Masculinity: A Critical Biography*, London, Unwin Hyman.

Kelly, A. (1985) 'The Construction of Masculine Science', *British Journal of the Sociology of Education*, no. 6, 133–54.

Kitwood, T. (1986) *Concern for Others: A New Psychology of Conscience and Morality*, London and New York, Routledge.

Kohlberg, L. (1981) *Essays in Moral Development*, New York, Wiley.

Labov, W. (1969) 'The Logic of Non-standard English', in Gigliogli, P. (ed.), *Language and Social Control*, Harmondsworth, Penguin.

Littleton, K. (1996) 'Girls and Information Technology', in Murphy, P. F. and Gipps, C.V., *Equity in the Classroom: Towards Effective Education for Girls and Boys*, London and Washington, Falmer Press.

Littleton, K. (1997) 'School Science' in Murphy, P.F. and Elwood, J., *Assessing Achievement*, London and Washington, Falmer Press.

Mac an Ghaill, M. (1994) *The Making of Men: Masculinities, Sexualities and Schooling*, Buckingham and Philadelphia, Open University Press.

MacLeod, D. (1997) 'Dog Eats Dog over Students', *Guardian Education Supplement*, 28 October.

Macrae, S., Maguire, M. and Ball, S.J. (1997) 'Whose "Learning Society"? A Tentative Deconstruction', Paper presented at School for Policy Studies, University of Bristol.

Mayall, B. (1994) 'Children in Action at Home and School', in Mayall, B. (ed.), *Children's Childhoods Observed and Experienced*, London, Falmer Press.

Measor, L. and Woods, P. (1984) *Changing Schools*, Milton Keynes, Open University Press.

Morrow, V. (1994) 'Responsible Children? Aspects of Children's Work and Employment Outside School in Contemporary United Kingdom', in Mayall, B. (ed.), *Children's Childhoods Observed and Experienced*, London, Falmer Press.

Morss, J. (1996) *Growing Critical: Alternatives to Developmental Psychology*, London and New York, Routledge.

Murphy, P.F. and Gipps, C.V. (1996) *Equity in the Classroom: Towards Effective Education for Girls and Boys*, London and Washington, Falmer Press.

Murphy, P.F. and Elwood, J. (1997) *Assessing Achievement*, London and Washington, Falmer Press.

National Curriculum Council (1990) *Education for Citizenship*, York, NCC.

National Curriculum Council (1991) *The English Curriculum*, York, NCC.

National Curriculum Council (1992) *Education for Citizenship*, York, NCC.

Pattman, R., Frosh, S. and Phoenix, A. (1998) 'Lads, Machos and Others: Developing "Boy-centred" Research', *Journal of Youth Studies*, no. 1 (2).

Pollard, A. (1985) *The Social World of the Primary School*, London, Cassell.

Qvortrup, J. (1991) *Children as a Social Phenomenon*, Budapest, Publicitas.

Rudduck, J., Chaplain, R. and Wallace, G. (eds) (1996) *School Improvement: What Can Pupils Tell Us?*, London, David Fulton.

Runnymede Trust (1994) *Multi-ethnic Britain: Facts and Trends*, London, Runnymede Trust.

Rutter, M., Maugham, B., Mortimore, P., and Ouston, J. (1979) *Fifteen Thousand Hours*, London, Open Books.

Salisbury, J. and Jackson, D. (1996) *Challenging Macho Values*, London and Washington, Falmer Press.

Sewell, T. (1997) *Black Masculinities and Schooling: How*

Black Boys Survive Modern Schooling, Stoke-on-Trent, Trentham Books.

Sharp, R. and Green, A. (1975) *Education and Social Control: A Study in Progressive Primary Education*, London, Routledge & Kegan Paul.

Skutnabb Kangas, T. (1988) 'Multilingualism and the Education of Minority Children' in Skutnabb Kangas, T. and Cummins, J. (eds) *Minority Education: From Shame to Struggle*, Avon, Multilingual Matters.

Smail, D. (1993) *The Origins of Unhappiness: A New Understanding of Personal Distress*, London, HarperCollins.

Stanworth, M. (1981) *Gender and Schooling*, London, Women's Research and Resources Centre.

Stanworth, M. (1983) *Gender and Schooling: A Study of Social Divisions in the Classroom*, London, Hutchinson.

Stoll, L., Myers, K. and Harrington, S. (1994) 'Linking School Effectiveness and School Improvement through Action Projects', Paper presented to Annual Conference, British Educational Research Association.

Tingle, S. (1985) *Going Mixed in ILEA: The English Curriculum*, London, English Centre Publication.

Tizard, B. and Hughes, M. (1984) *Young Children Learning*, London, Fontana.

Vygotsky, L. S. (1987) *The Collected Works of L. S. Vygotsky*, New York, Plenum.

Walden, R. and Walkerdine, V. (1985) *Girls and Maths: From Primary to Secondary Schooling*, London, Institute of Education Bedford Way Papers.

Walkerdine, V. (1981) 'Sex, Power and Pedagogy', *Screen Education*, no. 38, 14–21.

Walkerdine, V. (1988) *The Mastery of Reason: Cognitive Development and the Production of Rationality*, London, Routledge.

Walkerdine, V. (1990) *School Girl Fictions*, London and New York, Verso.

Ward, C. (1994) 'Opportunities for Children in Late Twentieth Century Britain', in Mayall, B. (ed.), *Children's Childhoods Observed and Experienced*, London, Falmer Press.

White, J. (1996) 'Research on English and the Teaching of Girls', in Murphy, P.F. and Gipps, C.V., *Equity in the Classroom: Towards Effective Education for Girls and Boys*, London and Washington, Falmer Press.

Whitty, G., Rowe, G. and Aggleton, P. (1994) 'Subjects and Themes in the Secondary School Curriculum', *Research Papers in Education* no. 14 (2), 159–81.

Willes, M. (1983) *Children into Pupils*, London, Routledge & Kegan Paul.

Wilmott, S. and Griffin, C. (1997) 'Wham Bam: Am I a Man?' *Feminism and Psychology*, no. 7 (1), 107–28.

Wood, D. (1988) *How Children Think and Learn: The Social Context of Cognitive Development*, Oxford and Cambridge, Mass., Blackwell.

Woods, P. (ed.) (1996) *Contemporary Issues in Teaching and Learning*, London and New York, Routledge.

Woods, P. (1977) 'Teaching for Survival', in Woods, P. and Hammersley, M. (eds), *School Experience*, Beckenham, Croom Helm.

Wright, C. (1987) 'Black Students, White Teachers', in Troyna, B. (ed.), *Racial Inequalities in Education*, London, Tavistock.

Index